THE FICTION WRITING HANDBOOK

The Professional Author's Guide to Writing Beyond the Rules

THE FICTION WRITING HANDBOOK

The Professional Author's Guide to Writing Beyond the Rules

Dario Ciriello

Published by Panverse Publishing
Alhambra, CA 91801

Visit us online at
www.panversepublishing.com

ISBN: 978-1-940581-86-6

PANVERSE
Panverse Publishing

TABLE OF CONTENTS

TABLE OF CONTENTS

TABLE OF CONTENTS

This book is dedicated to
Traci Morganfield, Bonnie Randall, and Doug Sharp,
fine writers and dear friends.

You all broke the rules and inspired me more than you know.

Foreword by Janice Hardy

There are those of you out there who have read multiple how-to books and advice on how to write, and none of it has resonated with you. Some of it might have even made you angry. It didn't work for you, and it didn't help your writing. You know deep in your core that your process and views on writing fall outside "traditional" advice and philosophies.

And this very likely frustrated you, because there was little out there to help you.

Which is why when Dario first told me about this book I thought it was a great idea—even though I disagree with his take on a lot (okay, most) of what's in it. Dario and I have vastly different opinions on how to write and develop a story, but we both agree on two fundamental things:

1. A story's job is to engage its readers.

2. How a writer chooses to do that is entirely up to him or her.

I've always been a firm believer that there is no right way to write. Every writer finds his or her path and develops their stories as they see fit. If one set of "rules" seems ridiculous to you, try another. Question what you do and why you do it. Understand the tools at your disposal and use them to tell the best story you can. What matters is the story, not the process in how a writer gets to it.

Two writers can disagree on that process and still agree with the results of that process. Dario uses examples in this book that criticize some of my favorite stories and extol the virtues of stories I thought were terrible. Yet we still respect each other as writers and understand that not every story is for every reader (or viewer). We can disagree and still value the effort a writer makes to tell a great story.

This is one reason writing can be such a pain in the butt—everything about it is open to interpretation. Opinions form beliefs, and beliefs create what we "know" to be true about writing and how to write a novel. And I guarantee you there's a writer out there who will tell you your belief is flat out wrong. Just as you no doubt believe some "rules" about writing are just as wrong.

Dario and I frequently think the other is wrong, and that's okay, because we're right about what really counts.

The story.

Find your process. Find your path. Tell your story. The rest of it will work itself out on the page.

—Orlando, FL, 2017

Author's Preface

The self-publishing and indie revolution has brought with it a deluge of writing books, websites, and blogs, most of which parrot the same, tired dogma to new writers desperate to publish by any means possible. Although there is plenty of excellent advice out there, so much of it is buried among mountains of generalization, dross, and sheer nonsense that a writer just learning their craft is likely to become confused and overwhelmed or else feel straitjacketed into churning out the same cookie-cutter fiction as everyone else.

This book is aimed at the newer and intermediate fiction writer who wants to develop an individual voice and style and understand the reasons underlying the so-called rules. A direct rebuttal of the formula-driven approach taken in the cult screenwriting book, *Save the Cat!*, this guide is intended as a discussion and collaboration between us, not a lecture. My objective is not to describe the tools and their basic uses but to help you see their limitations and help you apply these tools to your fiction with thought and discernment. Anyone can paint by numbers, but nobody's going to buy the result and hang it on their wall.

My approach, refined over fifteen years of writing, editing, publishing, and mentoring newer authors, is to question *all* conventional wisdom on the subject. Because of the tremendous influence of current fashions in screenwriting and film on every area of the publishing industry, from storytelling to production, and the fact that some of my readers will be screenwriters, I shall occasionally, especially in Part One, draw on examples from film as well as from literature to illustrate my point: literature or film, it's *all* storytelling.

A few basic components of craft—the different types of viewpoint, round vs. flat character, and other things easily found in scores of writing manuals and all over the web—may be only briefly mentioned in this book. However, where those basics are widely misrepresented or misunderstood, I'll try to clarify and redefine them. Anyone who reads and edits a lot of fiction sees the same errors and poorly-understood "rules" repeated ad infinitum.

If I leave some questions unanswered, this is intentional—I'm purposely not trying to lay down a raft of rules but to help you think and find your own way, and sometimes that's better done by offering pointers and hints rather than *diktats*.

You'll find a good deal of opinion in this book as we dig in, and perhaps disagree with some of it: that's okay. My purpose is to explore some issues from different angles and, occasionally, in greater depth than may be common, and in the process to raise questions and challenge assumptions. Good craft does matter and some few rules are necessary, but the vast majority are either dogma or passing fads. My point is that if you're good enough and know what you're about, you can do just about *anything* in your book. Literally. What matters is the reader experience. Everything else is secondary.

Whether your interest lies in genre or literary fiction, my goal is to help you tell *your* story in *your* voice and place it before your audience; to bring out your unique vision while adhering to the few rules that actually matter. If this book goes even some small way to achieving that, we've succeeded.

—Los Angeles, CA, 2019

ONE: RULES BE DAMNED

The main rule of writing is that if you do it with enough assurance and confidence, you're allowed to do whatever you like. (That may be a rule for life as well as for writing. But it's definitely true for writing.) So write your story as it needs to be written. Write it honestly, and tell it as best you can. I'm not sure that there are any other rules. Not ones that matter.

—Neil Gaiman

The Taliban Guide to Better Fiction

If you cruise writer and editor blogs on the web, you'll find a near-infinite series of posts with pumped-up titles like, "Zap Adverbs for Kick-Ass Prose!" "Thirteen More Ways to Kill Exposition," "Plot like a Hollywood Screenwriter," "Write for the Market," "The Seven Types of Subplot," and so on, a nightmare cornucopia of deranged dogma and rabid rules almost guaranteed to paralyze any new and impressionable writer.

Oh, please. What about, "Seven Shades of Stupid Advice," "The Wisdom of the Cookie-Cutter," "How Dare You Think for Yourself?!" and "The Taliban Guide to Better Fiction"? Now those are posts I'd like to see.

So let's talk babies and bathwater.

Writing, like any other craft, has some rules. And as we know, it's wise to learn and internalize these before breaking them. But it's also critical to know the limitations of rules and when to break them, and interpret most rules as guidelines rather than holy writ. No rule, as they say, should ever be followed off a cliff.

The problem for most beginning and intermediate writers lies in knowing where the cliff edge lies, where exceptions may be made, and—hardest of all—in attaining the correct distance to be able to look at their own work with some degree of objectivity.

Some rules—a very few—should be treated as inviolable. These include:

- Don't switch viewpoints in mid-scene (unless you're in omniscient)
- Don't resort to a deus ex machina at the climax to save your protagonist

- Don't bore the reader with lectures, trivial dialogue, excessive description, or anything else

- Always deal fairly with the reader and deliver on your promise to them

Pretty much everything else is negotiable. There is really only One Rule, One Rule to bind them all, and it is simply, *don't piss off the reader.*

Take adverbs, for instance. Although it's true that adverbs can flag vagueness and weaken prose, they exist for a reason. Consider the phrase, "She mostly agreed with him;" this might appear as internal dialogue in a character's head, and what it means is very clear—that she was in general but not complete agreement. The adverb (mostly) conveys the meaning with economy and minimum fuss, and any attempt to eliminate it will likely involve a good deal more wordage and burden our prose: or we could go down the uniquely silly path of replacing *mostly* with *pretty much* on the grounds that you eliminate the –ly adverb (insert eye roll here). Should we just eradicate it because some prose *mufti* has issued a *fatwa*? Of course not. This whole foofaraw about adverbs that began as good, rule-of-thumb advice has, after endless parroting, become a mindless mantra. I blame Hemingway, as I do for so much else.

Likewise with exposition, the cure is often worse than the disease. The key with exposition is to make sure it's both interesting and well-timed. Nobody wants a lecture; on the other hand, if the author's concern over infodumping borders on the obsessive —as it does for many—, readers will find themselves dissatisfied, even disoriented. I've closed and never reopened many a book, including some by Name authors, because of this. When readers need to know something, let them know it. Often the information can be slipped in deftly, but sometimes it's just more expeditious and painless to tell—yes, *tell*—the reader what they need to know rather than stand on your head trying to slip it in under the radar. If the desire for the information is there, the reader will welcome it. Voice can do miracles here, turning an indigestible lump of exposition into a delightful side-trip the reader will be happy to go along with.

And then the current preoccupation with redundancies, which has reached its zenith in the faddish crusade against the conjunction, "that" (e.g., "I think that it might be time."). I'm endlessly amazed that the same writing *muftis* who militate so strongly against this word appear entirely deaf to things like Hemingway's repeated, thudding "and". Yes, "that" is sometimes redundant but—like the serial comma—never does harm and is often useful for style, rhythm, flow, emphasis, and specificity. The lunatic obsession about leanness in prose right now reminds me more than anything of the starved supermodel look pioneered by British fashion model Twiggy in the 1960s: a thing of the moment, and not a healthy one. Fortunately, this too shall pass.

I'm a genre writer. Although I make every reasonable effort to write well and polish both story and prose over several revisions, my primary goal is to entertain the reader. I don't give a damn what the literary establishment thinks, or, for that matter, my more rule-obsessed peers: my goal is to deliver a story that's unique to me and which hooks the reader and keeps them turning pages, leaving them with a feeling of having been on a great ride when they finish the book. That's *what* counts. And anyone who believes that exposition and adverbs and an occasionally redundant word are going to kill a book needs a reality check. Write for your *readers*, not other writers.

The truth is that most readers are not writers, agents, or editors. They're not prose wonks. They aren't swayed by technical mastery or compliance with the latest fashion taught in the prose *madrassas*. Nor do they obsess over the question of whether a book neatly fits into a genre, category, or reader demographic. Readers want a good *story*, pure and simple. If you don't believe that, then I guess J.K. Rowling, John Grisham, Dan Simmons, Jacqueline Susann, E.L. James, Robert James Waller, Dean Koontz, Ayn Rand, Dan Brown, and Isaac Asimov's bestsellers were all just accidents. Because although some of these are good writers and others arguably mediocre, all of them have and do flout one or more of the "rules," flagrantly and often. Their readers love them, and it has not hurt their sales one bit.

In conclusion, I think part of being a professional in any field is to always question received wisdom. Yes, you certainly should learn the protocols and conventions; but slavish adherence to other people's dogma and assumptions not only limits your range, but also buys into what I believe is an unhealthy mindset. What's important is to tell your story in the way that best serves the reader.

In the end, the way you choose to interpret the barrage of writerly imperatives coming at you from every corner of the blogosphere is your own business. For myself, I've taken to laughing at most of it.

The Surrender of the New

Some years back, two news items on the excellent website io9 got me thinking about memes and the failure of the artistic imagination. The first of these concerned itself with aliens, the second with zombies. Only one really pissed me off. Here's why.

Annoying as it may be, the remarkable popularity of the zombie in popular culture is at least defensible in that the condition of the mythic undead correlates closely with a real-world phenomenon: rabies. As the io9 article pointed out, many of the symptoms, particularly the "silent, semi-lucid, unending aggression" of the rabies victim, are precisely those that typify the movie zombie. Well, fair enough. I still have sub-zero interest in reading or seeing movies about zombies, but I can buy them as somewhat believable, a pop-culture meme with some basis in fact.

The other news item was about a fourteen-minute short made for literally a zero budget. "This no-budget short film captures the creepiness of an alien encounter on a shoestring", trumpeted the io9 headline. Since I generally like this site, I decided to go with it and commit fourteen minutes of my time to see why this "science fiction film" (io9's words, not mine) was in the running for a grant from Ridley Scott's production company.

I should have known better.

This short, about a young woman whom nobody will believe trying to resist yet another alien visitation, is the worst kind of meme. Oh, the cinematography and production was fine, until the alien came along. At which point we're treated to bright white lights, electrical and electronic malfunctions, things rattling and shaking, and a three-fingered alien hand coming around the victim's bedroom door: in short, the generic alien encounter meme that has been around for well over three decades, at least since the movie *Close Encounters of the Third Kind*.

The pop culture meme of the skinny alien, with its childlike, elongated head, slitty eyes, three-fingered hands, blinding light, undampened electrical fields, and fond use of rectal probes, is out of control. But unlike zombies, we have no data point whatsoever on which to base the popular image of the alien's appearance: it's *made up*, people, and it wasn't a very good effort in the first place! The chance of aliens looking like this is no greater than aliens that look like octopi, or ambulatory potatoes, or nothing we can even begin to comprehend. And don't get me started on the stupid, unnatural, actinic blue lighting that for some unimaginable reason saturates humanity's future all the way to the heat death of the universe.

To my way of thinking, this is the worst kind of creative laziness. When you have the opportunity to do something entirely fresh and original—and science fiction provides that in spades—why does every filmmaker (and many writers!) do exactly the same thing that's been done before? If the answer is "because that's what audiences expect, and it sells", all I can do is slap the speaker and say the public deserves to be fleeced at every opportunity. You can tie a pink ribbon around a turd and put it in a Tiffany box, but it's still a turd. And yet, we continue to reward these pathetic, uninspired imitators.

Once in a very, very long while, a filmmaker comes along who gets it. Unfortunately, we have to go back even further than *Close Encounters* for that one, to the 1972 film (based on a 1961 novel), *Solaris*. Surreal? Hard to understand? You bet, and that's exactly the point, isn't it? A *real* alien encounter is going to be confusing and incomprehensible. And startlingly, memorably, original.

So the fact that hundreds of millions of people are convinced that the generic movie alien is representative of the real thing—as though we had even the shadow of a clue—is something I find both maddening and depressing. Haven't we been here with angels and fairies?

When an artistic form runs out of, or refuses to embrace, fresh ideas, it's usually considered dead. I think we can safely declare the science fiction genre in film—at least where aliens are concerned—to have entirely flatlined.[1]

The Stupid Never Stops

-Fit the First

In 1999, during a talk at MIT, the late, inimitable Douglas Adams quipped that "getting a movie made in Hollywood is like trying to grill a steak by having a succession of people coming into the room and breathing on it." I'm of the strong opinion that the book publishing industry, especially in the U.S., has for some years now been heading in the same dubious direction, a trend exacerbated by both macro-economic factors and the present turmoil within the industry.

Let me begin with my cards on the table: I'm biased. I prefer the real over the idealized, the purity of the artist's original vision over a heavily-massaged

---

1   At the time of writing there is one notable exception, the 2016 science fiction film *Arrival*, taken from the much better Ted Chiang novella, *Story of Your Life*. More like this, please, but leave out the gratuitous explosions, military porn, and end-of-the-world stakes added for the movie version.

corporate product; similarly, I believe true beauty is better appreciated without pancake makeup and every strand of immaculately-styled hair tucked perfectly in place. In the same way that a perfect world crafted by committee would be an intolerable, saccharin Disneyland, a book produced by committee with the cynical purpose of making the most bucks is not going to appeal to me. It may—*may*—be a smashing success, and that's okay if you want to live in a world of Dan Brown thrillers: I don't. I want some verisimilitude in a book, and that includes protagonists who sometimes aren't proactive, characters who might not change, and loose ends that don't get tied up in a pretty ribbon. The warped notion that an unholy alliance of agents, editors, accountants, and marketing people can somehow improve an already good book rather than turn it into processed mush is just laughable.

This isn't to say that developmental editing doesn't have a place: of course it does. As a freelance editor myself, I'd be a hypocrite to think otherwise. Even the best authors can be too close to their own work and will benefit from thoughtful, professional input. A good agent and editor can be an invaluable asset to any author. But the process has got entirely out of hand, with more books than ever being rejected or twisted out of shape because of the industry's near-religious faith in templates and formulas and their bizarre preoccupations over category, marketing demographics, and inherited assumptions of what readers want.

Don't believe me? Okay, let's return to science fiction in film. Those of you who read science fiction literature know very well that even the best stories and novels (Philip K. Dick, anyone?), in the process of being scripted and filmed, have most of their intelligent content ripped out and replaced with gunfights, explosions, chases, and slo-mo kung fu. Why? To target that all-important adolescent male demographic, of course.

In publishing, every one of us who works with authors or who is an author has seen this same progression. While I don't think we're quite at the woeful state of Hollywood, I believe the U.S. publishing industry is pretty far along the road to a lockstep conformity dictated by factors that have little to do with good writing and everything to do with perception and factors unrelated to quality.

Several years ago, at the World Fantasy Convention in San José, California, I asked Guest of Honor Zoran Živković why non-Anglophone or "World" science fiction typically has very different thematic concerns than U.S./U.K. science fiction, and is often far more vibrant, political, edgy, even surrealist. His reply was both insightful and telling: "The publishing industry in the U.S. is very powerful," he said, "and its strength is what determines the market. In the rest of the world, writers write what they want to write, not only what is marketable."

Award-winning science fiction author Aliette de Bodard, in a superb and heartfelt 2011 blog post_on the prevalence of U.S. tropes in storytelling, addresses the same issue from a slightly different angle:

> I'm tired of plots that value individualism and egotism above all else; of heroes that always have to be the masters of their own fates, to be active and not take anything that life deals at them lying down (whereas most of the time, we lie down, we accept, we deal with what we have been given); of heroes that have to be strong and only take marginal help from others to solve their own problems; of heroes that have a destiny, and of movies and books in which breaking up with all traditions is good so long as one finds and follow one's own path (there are a lot of cultures where breaking up with traditions isn't necessarily a good thing, and no, this doesn't mean that they're evil and backward). I'm tired of how genre(s) put(s) a disproportionate value on heroes who are active and not passive (and, by extension, belittles and dismisses every use of passive voice, and always asks for sentences to be frenetically punchy); of how the most important thing that can happen to a person is to be "given their own story," as [though] stories weren't made up of a mosaic of people all interacting together; of how teams exist only either as a background and foil for a single hero, or as a compendium of individuals, each fighting to outdo each other in stupid displays of heroism (yes, X-men, I'm looking at you).
>
> I'm tired of the casual acceptance of violence as a valid answer to anything, of the proliferation of guns in movies and books, of how it's always acceptable to go face the bad guys with a sword or a pistol instead of seeking a peaceful resolve. I am sick of the redefinition of narrative as violence, of how everything has to be a conflict in order to be valid—even to the point of defining conflict "against yourself," which contributes to trivializing the use of the word "conflict," not to mention twist it far beyond its original meaning. I don't want my stories to be only about blowing things up, or about good guys facing off bad guys, and dispatching them while stubbornly refusing to think about the ethics of killing, and the fact that the world seldom comes in black-and-white. I want violence to have consequences, both for those who have recourse to it, and for its victims;

not to be something you can shrug off in the morning as if it never happened.

I don't want stories in which the main character has to be sympathetic and with the moral high ground in order to be worthwhile; in which people have to change in order for the plot to be significant; in which women exist only to be sidelined or as surrogate men. I don't want stories that can be described in neat little boxes, or novels which can be reduced to a high concept and a series of story arcs (and, especially, I don't want to hear about the Hero's Journey, or the Three-Act Plot, or the Thirty-Six or Fifty-Five Basic Plots as if they were all some kinds of Holy Gospel). I want novels which can be complex and organic like life itself, and which don't have to be neatly pigeon-holed in order to be read and enjoyed.

In his near-cult book on screenwriting, *Save the Cat,*[2] Blake Snyder assures his readers that you must have conflict *in every scene* to keep the audience's attention. It's all about *the primal*, he tells us, insisting that "at its core, every scene in your movie must be as basic as this [death and sex] in order to get and keep the viewer's attention."

But wait! It seems that for a story to succeed, everything has to be rigidly structured and happen right on the beat, down to the page. Miss one of those beats or try for originality, and your chance of success, the cultists will tell you, goes down exponentially. A glance at the *Blake Snyder Beat Sheet* will tell you that the theme must be stated on page 5 of a script; that the catalyst occurs on page 12; that all is lost on page 75; and that the curtain comes down on page 110. "Isn't this pure? And easy?" the author tells us.

No. It's delusional tripe. A good writer whose voice and style is up to the job can describe the workings of a shoe factory and hold the reader spellbound.

This pressure to conformity, originating from purely commercial concerns, has warped the literary landscape, metastisizing like a cancer. Again, let me qualify: there's nothing wrong with the book industry attempting to pick winners and make a profit, but there's a great deal wrong with marketing people and accountants dictating a book's final shape; not only that, but—

2   *Save the Cat,* with its obsessive insistence on reducing everything to a formula and to measured beats, also has a near-religious following among authors, agents, and editors. Yet even when Snyder's prescription is followed to the letter, a great many novels and movies to which his template is applied fail miserably. How long before someone touts a pill or patent medicine guaranteed to make every book a bestseller?

like Hollywood—they've proven over and over that they're not very good at it, because otherwise every book would make a profit.

To conclude, not all artists or writers have 20-20 vision; there are plenty of bad indie books out there, just as there are plenty of bad indie movies. But, given a good cut of beef in the first place, I usually find that a steak seared and grilled on a good heat by an experienced hand tastes a great deal better than one cooked by having a succession of people breathe on it.

Fit the Second

A couple of years ago, my wife and I watched the 1997 science fiction film, *Contact*, again. And, like 95 percent of the science fiction movies I see, it annoyed the living hell out of me. Why? Because it was a cop-out.

The movie was a cop-out because it took no risks. In a genre where you can do anything, here was yet another contemptible example of the failure of imagination, the refusal to take risks. The movie fails largely by resorting to the same tired tropes: the ambitious politician, the evil, scheming intelligence baron, the attempt to reconcile the dichotomy between faith and science, the heavy-handed, tired message that humanity is at a crossroads between self-destruction and transformation. Oh, please. We knew all this half a century ago.

In trying to reduce the ineffable mystery of being to a comforting, human scale, the movie manages only one thing: to reassert traditional values and fill the viewer's mind with a bland mush—which, comforting as it may be to some, gets us nowhere. It's the modern equivalent of the heliocentric view of the world. Given the choice, I'd prefer to watch something truly awful, like *The Core* or *The Day After Tomorrow*, both of which are at least honestly and unpretentiously bad, and provide a good deal more entertainment value.

Contrast this with the 1971 Tarkovsky film, *Solaris* (not the 2002 remake with Clooney). Beyond being a daring, exceptional film by any standards, *Solaris* was true science fiction because it rejected convenient tropes and succeeded in communicating the inexplicable strangeness of the universe and the ultimate isolation of the human condition, rather than trying to simply comfort the viewer and rake in maximum bucks. *Solaris* was art; *Contact* was visual junk food. And no prizes for guessing which made the most money.

Publishing today has just about caught up with Hollywood. Art and vision long ago went out the window, taking theme and relevance with them. Few, if any, novels written by anyone of less than bestseller status get published without being heavily breathed on and hammered into formulaic conformity by several people, which likely include at minimum the author's agent, the publishing house's editor, and the marketing department. The result—at least in genre publishing—is an interminable deluge of fast-moving, cookie-cutter stories in which content is secondary to event and movement. If a story doesn't conform to the iron requirements of genre and category dictated by marketers; if a protagonist isn't relentlessly proactive; if the characters don't all change in direct conformity to the industry-standard character arc; if the ending doesn't resolve with all the main plot strands tidied up…forget it. Under these parameters, many of the world's greatest classics and most thoughtful, interesting novels wouldn't ever see print today.

Oh, there are exceptions, of course. Once in a while, a standout will get through, but those are very likely coming from an indie press or indie authors. And therein lies the only hope for risk-takers and nonconformist writers who put art, integrity, and theme front and center. Because if it doesn't fit the suffocating template of Big Publishing's category and genre obsession, it isn't going to be published. I know too many good writers, even agented, Name writers with excellent manuscripts, who don't stand a chance with the majors.

Let me illustrate my point with a little story about my own venture, Panverse Publishing.

Fit the Third

I started Panverse Publishing in 2009 because I wanted to provide a venue for new science fiction and fantasy writers working at novella length, a then rather underserved niche. As an example of how shortsighted even the relatively open science fiction market can be, I had the incredible fortune to be offered—and was delighted to publish—Ken Liu's searing novella, *The Man Who Ended History*, which went on to receive terrific reviews and was nominated for both the Hugo and Nebula Award. Everyone else had turned it down: how telling that it took an unknown to publish it.

After publishing three annual anthologies of five novellas each, stories from which garnered several award nominations and one win (The Sidewise Award for Alan Smale's 2010 novella, *A Clash of Eagles*, which went on to become a novel trilogy), I published my own nonfiction book, the bittersweet travel memoir titled *Aegean Dream*.

The manuscript of *Aegean Dream* had been with my then agent over a year; despite her best efforts and several nice notes from editors saying how they liked the writing, nobody would touch it because it (i) didn't conform to the saccharin *A Year in Such-and-Such* travel memoir formula, and (ii) at 135,000 words, it was at least 40 percent too long for the market category. I decided to publish it myself through Panverse.

With zero advertising and no bookstore presence, *Aegean Dream*, published in both digital and Print on Demand (POD) edition, sold almost 4,000 copies in 2012, was #1 book in both Greece categories on Amazon U.K. for over three months, and has now passed triple the average sales for a traditionally pubbed book. In addition, I was approached by Poland's largest travel book publisher, Pascal, who noticed its success in the U.K. and bought Polish language rights.

My bottom line? Readers, in my experience, are far smarter than most publishers give them credit for: they largely don't give a fig about all the formulas, templates, categories, and constraints the industry's barons and gatekeepers try to impose on them. Readers want a good book which is well-written, well-produced, and which, most of all, entertains them, period. And if it breaks a few "rules," and still works, all the better.

Fit the Fourth

Bear with me while I take you on one final trip here to round out this rant against groupthink and publishing by numbers before we get to the craft part.

Years ago, back in the 1970s, I used to ride motorcycles. My favorites were the British and Italian classics, the Triumph Bonneville and Norton Commando, and most of all, my beloved Ducati 750 Desmo. These were far from perfect machines: the Triumph left puddles of oil everywhere, the Norton had issues with its quirky Isolastic engine mounts, and my gorgeous Ducati suffered from maddening electrical issues. Nonetheless, each of these beasts had at least one feature so outstanding, did one thing so divinely well, that I could overlook all their faults.

By contrast, when I got my first Japanese motorcycle, the newly-introduced Honda CB 750, a four-cylinder technological marvel of the time, I experienced a strong sense of anticlimax: from handling to acceleration to braking, the bike did everything well; it didn't drip oil, didn't try to shake itself—and you—to pieces, and it was dependable in the way we've now come to expect from everything Japanese and German. But I didn't *love* it. I couldn't: it lacked spirit, the one outstanding trait that redeemed all the faults of my previous European machines. Why?

Design by committee.

Three decades later, I still feel the same way. It seems a universal law that if you try to iron out every flaw in something and take a truly cooperative approach to design or creativity, the end result lacks heart, spirit, fire, passion, whatever you want to call it. (I'm sure you're thinking right now of examples that would prove me quite wrong, but I'm afraid you'll never convince me. I have a seventh sense that can discern genius and creative fire in anything, from a frying pan to an aircraft).

To make something that works very well is easy; to make something that turns ordinary people into fanatical cultists (see: Mac owners) is far harder. Apple trumps HP or Dell any day when it comes to heart and passion—and this from someone firmly in the PC/Microsoft camp.

This is true in all the arts. All things being equal (in this case, the writer being good at their craft and having a good story to tell) I'd far rather read the story at least close to the way the writer originally envisaged it, at the length they felt it needed to be, complete with the ambiguous or unhappy ending the publisher's marketing department vetoed because it could hurt sales, than a heavily-massaged, corporate product which half a dozen people have had major input on.

This isn't to say that writers don't need input. I understand the myopia all writers, myself included, can suffer, and God knows we all need feedback and copyediting. But I believe that when the corporate approach is applied to creativity, something is going to get lost—a quality, perhaps intangible, that makes the work unique and sings of the artist's spirit and vision.

And, dig: can you imagine an art dealer or gallery owner walking into an artist's studio and telling them more people would like the painting and it would fetch a higher price if they backed off the Prussian Blue a bit and made the canvas taller and narrower? Painters are typically left to work undisturbed, and the finished product is the way *they* see it.

We've seen what the corporate approach to art has done for Hollywood and the music industry (and before that, the brewing industry when it was dominated by just a few huge corporations like Budweiser) over the decades, and it's not pretty: it's sucked all the uniqueness and bite from the products of each and incrementally replaced them with a formulaic smoothness that's wholly lacking in originality and...integrity? Fire? Truth? Consider Tolkien's books, the *Firefly* TV series, the movie *Psycho*; would any of those have turned out the way they did if the creative genius behind each had been replaced by a committee and second-guessed at every turn?

For a compelling example in music, consider John Mellencamp's superb 2010 album, *No Better Than This*, recorded the way they used to do it in the 'fifties, with everyone singing and playing around a single microphone. As Mellencamp explains, "everything was cut live with no overdubs or studio, nothing! These are real songs being performed by real musicians—an unheard-of process in today's world. Real music, for real people!" Smooth, it's not. But it's drenched in integrity, spirit, and that unmistakable, ineffable spark of creative truth.

Is it any coincidence that each of those industries—Hollywood, the music industry, and the breweries—have now lost huge amounts of market share to indies in each of those fields? The worm turns.

Yeah, I can hear all the rebuttals, but, hey—this is op-ed, not a statistical analysis. And, yeah, I've always been an autodidact and a loner in every one of my endeavors, winning or losing largely on my own merits. It's the way I'm wired. I'll take advice, even solicit it, but in the end I'll do it *my* way. And so should you.

When you have a seventh sense, you have to trust it. Even if it means leaving a few drips of oil here and there.

ᗆ

TWO: THE BASIC PARTS

Writerly dogma is like fake news: it chases the real thing away. In many years of critiquing and editing, it's become very clear to me that while the RVLES get chiseled deep into every writer's skull, people can spend years writing but still not understand what actually matters. Let's try to untangle it all in this section.

Story

What *is* a story?

A story is the recounting of a chain of events for entertainment and/or transmitting meaning. We tell stories to teach, to amuse, and to make sense of events, including tragic and devastating ones.

In the course of storytelling, meaning is sometimes created from whole cloth, even from previously unconnected events. The events in a story may have no causal connections, but humans are pattern-seekers, and will look for and find patterns even when there are none.

Unfortunately, story and plot have become rather conflated in recent decades, and a good many writers (and, worse, writing teachers and gurus) have lost sight of the fact that although a story may have a plot, it does not *need* one to be a story. Plot happens when the writer or storyteller draws lines between events to establish causal links between them. Several famous authors have expressed this in different ways, but the matter is a simple one: plot is what *happens* in a story, the causal sequence of events. A story is what the novel, movie, or whatever is *about*.

And yet (we'll go into this again when we discuss *theme*), ask a person what a book is about, and there's every chance they'll launch off into a protracted description of the story events—i.e., the plot.

This occurs because we're hardwired to look for patterns and causality to begin with: it's an evolutionary survival mechanism. But plot gets twisty and complicated, whereas a story is a simple thing. Let's take *Lord of the Rings* as an example most of you will know.

The Story: Lord of the Rings is the tale of a simple hobbit whose quiet life is overturned when he finds himself the keeper of the One Ring, an artifact of immense power, and of the ensuing quest to destroy it.

The Plot: Frodo the hobbit inherits a golden ring from his uncle Bilbo on the occasion of their joint birthday. When Gandalf the wizard tells Frodo that this pretty bauble is actually the One Ring fashioned by Sauron, the Dark Lord of Mordor, Frodo is horrified. Gandalf tells him to keep the ring secret and promises to return soon. But when Frodo receives a letter from Gandalf telling him to leave the Shire and...

Yes, we could go on for pages. Story—what the tale is about—is simple. Plot isn't.

Some people are born storytellers. These are the people who as children created imaginary, complex worlds and interactions for their dolls or action figures far beyond the more simple, imitative play of other kids, often narrating it all as they played (the Brontës set the gold standard here). They're the fortunate ones—the rest of us have to learn.

One caution: when developing your story idea, it's critical to go deep and look hard at that which comes too easily. We each have this cluttered attic of a brain overflowing with images, tropes, and clichés accumulated over years of living, reading, watching TV and movies, playing RPGs (Role Playing Games), and so on. That stuff is all used, secondhand, off-the-shelf. And while there's not much new under the sun, the first stuff likely to fall on your head the moment you open the trapdoor to that attic looking for ideas, characters, settings, or plot events, is tired junk.

It's important therefore to recognize that those first ideas for setting and character are often stock, used goods. Set them aside. As any author's partner can attest, we spend a lot of our time lost in thought or staring at walls. There's a good reason for this: we're digging, thinking, reaching down into the well, making patterns and cutting whole cloth for our bespoke clothes rather than just shopping at the thrift store. Make that brain *work*.

Now that we're clear about what a story is, we can begin to look at the component parts which most stories, certainly the vast majority of them, will require.

Character

The first thing to understand is that every character in a work of fiction must be clear, solid, and absolutely believable. Unless the author has their characters in sharp focus, the reader never will.

This is important to point out because at the outset of crafting a new work, the writer is unlikely to have their main characters in full, clear focus. Typically we have (and had better have!) a general idea of who they are from the outset, but it's only as we forge ahead into the story, confronting them with challenges and watching how they interact with one another, that we finally begin to understand our characters at a deep level.

For example, when I start writing, I may know that Sara, my protagonist, was born in the Hudson River Valley in March 1987, that she works in sales at a pharmaceutical corporation, and is a vegetarian. She's never married, has a black lab, and likes trance and techno music. I know her hair color, her star sign, and that she suffers mild claustrophobia; although a semi-practicing Catholic, she nonetheless likes to party and has more than once woken up next to a stranger, so thank goodness for confession. I know her loves and virtues, her unconscious conflicts, her darkest secrets.

This is all helpful in getting my story rolling, but knowing a bunch of facts about Sara doesn't mean that I know who she really is, and specifically how she'll interact with others or behave in a given situation. All these things we list on character sheets at the planning stages of a novel are surface observations, physical characteristics, general character traits. Sara is all there in potential, but she's not breathing yet: it's only as the story progresses that she comes fully alive and shows me who she really is—and if I'm doing my work well, she's sure to surprise me by revealing aspects of herself I hadn't seen and behaving in ways I couldn't have predicted…*but which all ring absolutely true.*

So whether you're an outliner or not, it's only as your story gets underway and your characters begin to have meaningful, detailed interactions in the story world that you really begin to know them in the way you know people in the everyday world we inhabit. In the process, your characters will (hopefully) do things that will require adjustments in the earlier part of the story, when you were writing about them at only the surface level. In fact, it's often only when the first draft is done and has cooled and you reread it prior to starting your revision work that you can grasp your characters entirely, in the round.

The second essential of writing character is that the reader *must* care. If you fail to make the reader care (and quickly) about the characters and what happens to them, all is lost. It's that important.

Note that the caring can go in either direction, love or hate; in fact, one of the greatest joys of my writing career to date was when an author I enormously respect said of Dafyd Jones, the villain in my novel *Black Easter,* "I hated this bastard with every cell in my body [...] I hated how Dafyd won all the time and was angered that his smug above-it-all bullshit never received any comeuppance…until the end."

Making a reader care is not that hard. The ace in the author's hand when a reader opens the book is that the reader *wants* to believe, wants to enjoy the ride. It's not so much what the writer does as what they *don't* do that sometimes makes the difference. The reader is on your side until you trip them up. All they're asking is that you tell a good story about interesting people who feel real to them.

The key is that little word: *real*. When a reader starts a novel, they know very well that the characters in it aren't real people, and that everything they do (unless you're writing, say, historical fiction) is made up. The reader has agreed to *suspend disbelief* in order to enjoy the story.[3]

How then, does the writer make their characters real to the reader? To begin with, we incorporate traits and details drawn partly from observation and partly from imagination. Characters aren't always spun from whole cloth. It's natural to base a character, especially a sympathetic one, on someone we know, but we also need to mix in thread and dyes of our own choosing in order to make them unique (and perhaps avoid lawsuits). And then we have to nuance them further, making sure that our protagonists have flaws and our villains, virtues.

We live surrounded, almost crushed at times, by people, real and imaginary. Our hearts and minds are so saturated with them that we can immediately distinguish the traits of well-drawn characters from cardboard ones. Speech, mannerisms, creativity, likes and dislikes, humor or lack thereof, obsessive behaviours…. All these things combine to make us unique. When a reader recognizes this "faithful adherence to the truth of nature," to use Coleridge's phrase, they cannot help but care, *unless* the author does something to break the spell.

And yet many writers—not only beginners but even some popular bestselling authors—appear to do all the above and yet still fail to make the reader

---

3   The term was first coined by the poet Samuel Taylor Coleridge following a conversation with neighbor and fellow poet William Wordsworth in which they agreed upon "the power of exciting the sympathy of the reader by a faithful adherence to the truth of nature." Coleridge expanded this by writing in 1817 (my boldface), "[…] my endeavors should be directed to persons and characters supernatural, or at least romantic, yet so as to transfer from our inward nature a human interest and a semblance of truth sufficient to procure for these shadows of imagination that **willing suspension of disbelief** for the moment, which constitutes poetic faith."

care deeply about their characters and, consequently, the story's outcome.

You might ask yourself how this is possible when the author is a bestseller; I contend that most of these frigid tomes fall in the tech/war porn thriller genre read mostly by men who normally read no other fiction, and which rely instead on their appeal to a tired, cookie-cutter patriotism served up with a surfeit of action, violence, technical detail, and formulaic political intrigue. Their readers may continue to turn pages, but they'd probably be just as riveted by the evening news on network TV. The rest of us want something better crafted.

So what's the difficulty? Generally, newer writers often just haven't got the craft part down yet; with seasoned writers of the type mentioned above, the failure to make the reader care seems a product of a peculiar kind of laziness, arrogance, or perhaps a simple lack of empathy. Maybe that's why so many of them write war porn. Each to his own.

For an example of an author who writes spy novels and geopolitical thrillers yet really gets character, take John Le Carré, author of *The Spy Who Came in from the Cold, The Night Manager, The Tailor of Panama,* and the superb George Smiley series, among many other novels. Unlike the macho adrenalin pushers mentioned above, Le Carré's work sucks you in by degrees, building reader investment until you're so deeply absorbed in the characters and their interactions that you feel as emotionally aligned with the story world as with your own everyday life. In *Tinker, Tailor, Soldier, Spy,* there's a remarkable sequence of static scenes several pages long during which Smiley simply sits in a dingy hotel room reading old files from decades ago; in the hands of many authors, this would quickly result in the reader closing the book; in Le Carré's hands, these scenes are riveting, compelling, and emotionally intense.

Le Carré and other writers of his calibre know that it's not enough to simply incorporate the traits of real people into your characters: you have to draw the reader into the characters' heads and make them see the world through their eyes, walk in their shoes. The writer does this by using *interiority*, about which much more in a later chapter.

It's worth pointing out that a character—let's call them "B"—can be equally well portrayed by establishing another credible character ("A") and showing B through A's eyes and feelings. This technique can be especially potent in the case of a character whom the writer may want to keep ambiguous in the reader's eyes, at least for a time. Romance authors excel at this technique.

This method of approaching one character through the perceptions of another whom the reader already knows and trusts can accomplish a great deal of heavy lifting, especially when the viewpoint is slathered with attitude and judgment. Take this passage from science fiction author C.J. Cherryh's *Rider at the Gate*, in which one of the main characters, young Danny Fisher, sees Guil Stuart, an intense and haunted high-country rider:

> *In that time-stretched moment he realized he knew Stuart—knew him for a fair man, borderer, true, but never the bullying sort: far from it, Stuart had sat on a rainy spring evening on Gate Tavern's porch, sharing three drinks with a kid who, at that time, could only pay for one, and telling a towner brat who'd dared—dared—come to a borderer to ask how he could ever hope to get the long-distance convoy jobs he dreamed of.*

In just a single paragraph, the author has given us a deep insight into Stuart's humanity and character without even bringing him onstage, as well as deepening the reader's understanding of young Danny, through whose viewpoint this character insight is delivered. The specific detail coupled with Danny's honest self-assessment ("a towner brat who'd dared"), leaves us in no doubt that this is a judgment we must accept as fair and true.

Finally, it's important to note that characters can be fully believable even when doing unbelievable things: if that weren't the case, we'd have no paranormal romance, no science fiction, no fantasy, no James Bond films. So long as the character is well-drawn and internally consistent, they will be believable to the reader; and if the story world allows for magical spells or lightsabers, the reader will buy it. In fact, the reader will buy it even when the story world doesn't allow it, which is why Bram Stoker went to so much trouble to have Van Helsing, once he was established as a believable character, persuade Seward and the other men that Lucy is one of the "un-dead:" skepticism—within reason—when faced with the fantastic is a characteristic all of us share, or at least recognize.[4]

Ω

---

4   From *Dracula*, Ch. XV: DR. SEWARD'S DIARY—continued:

This turned my blood cold, and it began to dawn upon me that I was accepting Van Helsing's theories; but if she were really dead, what was there of terror in the idea of killing her? He looked up at me, and evidently saw the change in my face, for he said almost joyously:—

"Ah, you believe now?"

I answered: "Do not press me too hard all at once. I am willing to accept."

On Emotion

New writers often struggle to portray emotion. The key word here is *struggle*: typically, a writer who hasn't yet got a real handle on craft exaggerates everything, trying to wrestle and cajole the reader into feeling. The result, at best, is melodrama.

The only way to make the reader *feel* and to show a character's emotional journey is, again, to make that character solid and believable. Once this is accomplished, if your character has some good qualities, even virtues—and your protagonists had better have some—the reader will align to some degree with them, at which point the reader cannot help but feel for your protagonist as they encounter challenges, reversals, pain, and heartbreak. You can't force a reader to care and feel without doing the work required to make the character believable and likeable, at which point no manipulation is required: the reader will react spontaneously without any applied pressure.

As an example, take the scene in *Pride and Prejudice* where Darcy, in the grip of intense feelings he cannot control or understand, declares his passionate love to Elizabeth and in the process shows his disregard and utter contempt for her family and social standing: as we read the scene, everything that is good in us reaches out to Elizabeth as she listens in shock and disbelief. And her rejoinder, which cuts so deeply, only serves to underscore her pain. The reader, fully aligned by now with Elizabeth through Austen's brilliant character work, and, at this point, somewhat fascinated by Darcy, can't help but feel as she feels, react as she reacts. Austen does nothing here to manipulate the reader, never tells us how to feel: she simply gives us dialogue and limpid interiority. The exchange, taken out of context, is relatively mild and undramatic. What makes the scene, occurring as it does more than halfway through the work, an emotional gut punch for the reader is everything that has gone before and brought us into such close alignment with Elizabeth.

(Darcy begins)

"But disguise of every sort is my abhorrence. Nor am I ashamed of the feelings I related. They were natural and just. Could you expect me to rejoice in the inferiority of your connections? To congratulate myself on the hope of relations, whose condition in life is so decidedly beneath my own?"

Elizabeth felt herself growing more angry every moment; yet she tried to the utmost to speak with composure when she said,

"You are mistaken, Mr. Darcy, if you suppose that the mode of your declaration affected me in any other way, than as it spared me the

concern which I might have felt in refusing you, had you behaved in a more gentleman-like manner."

On Protagonists

How virtuous does a character need to be for the reader to align with them and care about their trials? They shouldn't be a goody two-shoes who strides through the story trying for sainthood: that's more likely to make your reader gag than elicit their empathy.

For me, there's no better guide to the moral core of a good protagonist than what I think of as the "Chandler Rule," from Raymond Chandler's "mean streets" essay in the November 1945 issue of *The Atlantic Monthly*:

> *[...] down these mean streets a man must go who is not himself mean, who is neither tarnished nor afraid. The detective in this kind of story must be such a man. He is the hero, he is everything. He must be a complete man and a common man and yet an unusual man. He must be, to use a rather weathered phrase, a man of honor—by instinct, by inevitability, without thought of it, and certainly without saying it. He must be the best man in his world and a good enough man for any world.*

I recommend reading this quote more than once and taking it to heart: you won't find a better guide to building your protagonist anywhere. Every clause luminously illustrates and encapsulates precisely the traits of a good protagonist.

First, the hero, the protagonist, is both common (relatable) and unusual. They're a person of honor who retains a certain humility—they *can't* be anything else, this is the way they're wired. A trustworthy, honest person, the real deal.

But most important of all perhaps is the last phrase: *He must be the best man in his world and a good enough man for any world.* This directly addresses the question of moral relativism; in a story set in a corrupt, decaying, or dystopian world, our hero shines and blazes bright—they are the best in that world. But at the same time, they're good enough that if you were to put them into a story set in a kinder world full of light and goodness, they'd hold their own and not appear tarnished.

On Antagonists

Your antagonist is no different. If you want the reader to take them seriously enough to dislike them, to want them to lose, even to hate them (and by extension care about who prevails), the same rules apply: you *must* make the character believable.

It's been said that everyone's the hero in their story. We're fortunate to live in an age in which writers and readers mostly recognize this truth, with the happy result that black-and-white, two-dimensional heroes and villains don't get much traction (we could quibble over Dan Brown's *The Da Vinci Code*, but I'll spare you the rant). It will help bring your wicked antagonist to life if you grace them with some virtues such as courage, honesty, or the capacity for love. Adolf Hitler loved his mother; Hermann Göring was a conservationist.

The traits that make an antagonist dislikeable should also be common, recognizable ones, though your villain will surely take them to excess. We all live on a continuum, each of us a complex balance of virtue and vice. The best vices of course are those we recognize and despise in ourselves: jealousy, pride, arrogance, greed, and so on. The inability in an antagonist to empathize, to understand and share another's feelings and motives, is almost a given; a character who possesses empathy but whose other vices (greed, lust, etc.) override it, will still make a good villain—in fact, a better one by virtue of their complexity. We may all be fashioned from the same cloths and dyes, but I submit that most real people are never lacking in interest, contrast, and texture.

In Conclusion

Character is the underpinning of story. It can be seen as a dynamic web of relationships and dependencies, each part meshing with and affecting the others. When married to the dynamic webs of other characters in the work, the whole works together to give life to the plot and determine the direction, sequence, and outcome of story events.

Without character there is no plot, no story, no drama, no comedy, no tragedy. Character and plot must form a seamless whole for the story to work: neither exists in a vacuum, and the plot vs. character, genre vs. literary fiction argument is essentially a specious and unhelpful one. Everything flows from character in action.

Homer and Shakespeare understood these basics, and so must we.

Q

Viewpoint

So much has been written on viewpoint that I'm not going to dive deep on this one, but it must be mentioned.[5] Here's a brief summary definition of possible viewpoints *aka* VP or Point-of-View (PoV):

First person. "I." The entire story is told through the viewpoint character's eyes. Classic examples of this approach include Mark Twain's *The Adventures of Huckleberry Finn* and Sir Arthur Conan Doyle's *Sherlock Holmes* series (told entirely from Dr. Watson's PoV).

Second person. "You." Everything is written as though the reader were the PoV character. My only comment on this technique is to leave it alone unless you really know what you're doing. It's hardly ever necessary and can feel very manipulative. Ted Chiang's 1998 novella, *Story of Your Life,* which went on to become the 2016 movie, *Arrival,* is one of the extremely rare cases in which second person PoV is both justified and applied with exceptional skill.

Third Person. The most common style in contemporary writing, third person PoV breaks down into two main branches:

(i) Third Person Limited (Single). "He/She." All the events are seen and told through the eyes of one character; this technique is similar to first person but the third person pronoun is used. J.K. Rowling's *Harry Potter* series is (with a very few slips) written in this PoV.

(ii) Third Person Limited (Multiple). "He/She." The reader experiences the story through the eyes of multiple alternating characters but *never within the same scene.*

Omniscient (aka "God's Eye View"). Everything is seen and told by an external narrator who can dive into any character's head and see through their eyes at any time. Tolkien's *Lord of the Rings* is a terrific example of this technique.

It's worth noting that some writers, either through mastery or clumsiness, blur the lines and occasionally dance on the edge between omniscient and third person limited. Stephen King sometimes does this so smoothly you don't see his hands move, giving us the overwhelming majority of a novel in third limited and then opening up the God's eye view just once or twice for a few lines or a paragraph to tell us something the PoV character(s) couldn't possibly know.

---

5   For a more detailed discussion of PoV basics, there are a number of excellent books on the topic, and of course thousands of pages of material freely available on the web.

Once you have a solid grasp of PoV, don't be afraid to experiment with it and try different effects, so long as you keep control and have a plan. You are God in your novel: you can do anything you like, so long as you have the skill to pull it off.

Picking the correct viewpoint for your novel and—unless you're writing in first person or omniscient—for each individual chapter or scene is critical. If you're writing in third person limited (multiple), some of the most important considerations influencing your viewpoint choice will be:

- Is the character important enough to merit a viewpoint?
- Does the character have a lot at stake during the scene? They should.
- How will the character's presence affect the events of the scene?
- Does this character's viewpoint add suspense and help information management by showing things other characters don't see?

The viewpoint character chosen will also affect the *tone* of the scene (more on tone later in the book).

Setting and Description

A common error among newer writers is failure to anchor the action in a solid, well-drawn setting. The writer needs to supply enough specific detail to set the scene, painting a clear picture in the reader's mind. If whatever is going on appears to be taking place in a white room or, equally bad, a generic or stereotype setting, the hook will be blunted. You don't need a lot of description, but you do need to *own* the setting.

The overwhelming majority of adults in the 21st century have watched countless movies and TV shows, and our minds are literally overflowing with pictures. A New York penthouse? Got it in mental image repository. A medieval village? Check. An orbiting space station? No problem. A sprawling, crime-ridden shantytown on the outskirts of Rio or Calcutta? Been there, seen it.

Your job as a writer is to make the setting uniquely yours, painting a clear picture in the reader's mind rather than forcing them to reach for something already in their mental catalogue of stock images. To do less is sheer laziness and will hobble your story from the beginning.

With description, less is generally more. I usually like to paint in the setting with two or three quick, broad brushstrokes and one sharp, closely-observed detail to bring the image into crisp focus, make it pop.

Even when you're describing something that seems everyday, like an industrial building, you need to *own* it, make it yours. From my first novel, *Sutherland's Rules*:

> It was a brief cab ride from the ferry terminal to Henk's warehouse, a new-looking, light industrial building in cool greys broken by a broad, off-center designer stripe of bright orange. Watching Billy knock on the small door next to the roller shutter, Christian had an overwhelming sense of déjà vu, Mazar all over again, but in what felt like a different century.

If I've done my work correctly, the reader isn't looking at just a generic light industrial building, they're seeing *mine*, complete with the off-center orange stripe and the small door just where I said it was.

You should also try to engage more than one of the senses. From my novel, *Black Easter,* the opening of chapter five:

> The rowboat nosed up as it ran aground on the harbor beach with a growl of displaced pebbles. The two sailors shipped their oars and Otto, Klaus's aide, was first ashore, hand extended to help him disembark. Klaus, still deeply nauseous from the sea voyage, stood unsteadily and allowed himself to be assisted. It was cool, and the thickening clouds promised rain.

The broad strokes: a rowboat with the characters inside; a sea beach and harbor; cool air. The growl of pebbles as the rowboat runs ashore provides specific detail and auditory dimension. The cool air engages the sense of touch. I could have added something about the smell of rain, or perhaps rotting fish, to bring in the olfactory dimension, smell being the most evocative sense. Still, it works well enough to ground the reader without boring them.

I'm not big on describing characters, and tend to go light on details of appearance; again, a couple of broad strokes and maybe just one or two closely-observed specific details. This from an early short story of mine, *Valley of the Shadow*; we're in the protagonist's viewpoint:

> Seated alone across the terrace and two tables back was an attractive, sharp-featured woman, a little angular about the shoulders, self-confident in her bearing. She had short black hair, and her long bones fit interestingly in tailored jeans and a lightweight black leather jacket.

In conclusion, then:

- Keep description brief and interesting

- Make your description pop with at least one specific detail

- In tight viewpoint (interiority), description can and should also tell us something about the viewpoint character, their mood, and so on, by both the elements they focus on and their appended judgment and feelings

- Try to avoid generic words and images

- Own every setting

Setup

The next essential to a strong story after rounded characters and picking the right viewpoint is a strong initial setup. Some of the most powerful setups are the simplest: all you need is a protagonist (or antagonist) with a problem.

To see this simplicity at work, one need look no further than popular songs. For a terrific setup, you'd be hard pressed to beat the opening verses of the Charlie Daniels Band's hit song, *The Devil Went Down to Georgia.*[6]

- In the first four lines—just thirty-one words—we already have the antagonist and his goal: the Devil, behind on recruiting his quota of souls, has come to Georgia willing to bargain

- The following two lines (fifteen words) sketch in Johnny, our protagonist, whom the Devil sees playing a fiddle with great skill

- Two more lines, a mere nine words, give us a visual setting to anchor the scene as the Devil jumps onto a tree stump

- In the following seven lines (fifty-six words) the Devil sees an opportunity and takes his chance; a skilled fiddler himself, he makes his challenge and the stakes are declared: a solid gold fiddle against Johnny's immortal soul

- Another three lines, twenty-seven words in all, complete the opening when Johnny accepts the Devil's challenge.

---

6   For copyright reasons, I'm not reprinting the lyrics here, but if they're not already stuck in your head they can be immediately found online.

The setup is complete. The story is on its way, all this accomplished in a total of 146 words, less than half the average paperback page. It's all there, settings, goals, motivations, and conflict. And as a final flourish, the songwriter has even given us a glimpse into Johnny's prideful character, which only increases his jeopardy and our sense of the stakes. What if taking the Devil's challenge and gambling his soul *is* a sin? What if Johnny's not as good as he thinks he is?

A strong setup is usually powered by the most basic human drives or passions: fear, love, need for security or recognition, hunger; certainly by violating the Biblical commandments or committing any of the Bible's seven deadly sins[7]...okay, *sloth* might be a hard one for a setup, but if used to power internal conflict or arouse another principal character's emotion, you can even make that work.

Setups often fall into story types, or *tropes*. Above, we have the classic *deal with the devil*, a type of tale that has been around for millennia. The *uncollected debt*, which I used to drive my first novel, *Sutherland's Rules,* is another. The fact that a setup falls into a well-used trope in no way weakens it—in fact, quite the opposite: oft-repeated story types, like character archetypes, are laced deep into our psyche and freighted with a mythic power all their own.

And there are only so many story types available (various people have come up with differing numbers ranging from one[8] to three, four, five, six, seven, and up to at least twenty-six, rather like physicists trying to pin down the number of possible dimensions as they struggle to refine their understanding of the real). My personal guideline is the three-type breakdown I touched on earlier, which is:

- Man against man

- Man against nature

- Man against himself

(Note that these are old and classic definitions, and no offense should be taken at my failure to use gender-neutral language. I am quoting here, not coining.)

A trope occurring in a setup or within a story (most stories contain many tropes) is not the same as a template or beat-driven formula which someone tries to apply to an entire novel to mold it by force into a perceived "bestseller" or "blockbuster".

---

7   Faith neither required nor endorsed: I'm using the Bible here as a universal list on which many societies base their system of laws, and as keys to the human heart and mind insofar as driving fiction is concerned.

8   "There is one story and one story only / that will prove worth your telling" –Robert Graves, *To Juan at the Winter Solstice.*

Let's consider just a few more examples of great setups and their plot-driving passions/motivators:

- A driven young scientist tries to create a living human being from inanimate body parts (Mary Shelley, *Frankenstein*: deadly sin #4, *hubris*, pride)

- A young prince seeks revenge on his uncle for murdering his father to take his wife and throne (William Shakespeare, *Hamlet*: Hamlet's uncle manifests at least three of the seven deadly sins— envy, lust, and greed—as well as breaking three of the Ten Commandments by killing, stealing, and coveting)

- The captain of a whaling ship becomes obsessed by his quest for revenge on the white whale that bit off his leg (Herman Melville, *Moby Dick*: deadly sin #6, wrath)

- A young boy escapes from his drunken father and runs away in search of freedom and adventure (Mark Twain, *The Adventures of Huckleberry Finn*: universal yearning for freedom and new experience in a story world where sins and transgressions abound)

Dialogue

The single most important thing about dialogue is that it should flow and feel natural—but not *too* natural. As anyone who's ever transcribed an interview knows, real speech is so full of tics and fillers, "umms" and "errs" and "likes" that it would be almost unreadable, and certainly annoying, on the page.

In fiction, the best dialogue is an idealized, distilled essence of real-world speech. It's naturalistic, giving the full illusion of realism. At the same time, however, fictional dialogue has some heavy lifting to do. Every line of dialogue in a work of fiction needs to do at least one, preferably more, of the following:

- Be realistic
- Advance the plot
- Deliver information
- Reveal character
- Shed light on relationships between characters

A Couple of Basics

Although dialogue tags—adverbial or otherwise—are a very basic part of writing, even skilled writers make mistakes here. So let's just remind ourselves of a few fundamentals, those items every editor sees so often as to make them climb the walls.

First, help your reader keep track of speakers during a long exchange by tagging one or the other with a gesture or speech tag (*he/she* said) every four or five lines: few things are more frustrating for a reader than having to read back up and figure it out, and in some conversations they won't be able to tell at all. When there are more than two speakers, it may be necessary to tag every line of dialogue.

Second, try to minimize use of adverbial tags (descriptors ending in *–ly*) to support dialogue tags. There *are* occasions when it may be the most economical and transparent way to convey meaning (e.g., *she said softly* can be more elegant than *she said, lowering her voice to a murmur*), but on the whole, the adverbial tag is a craven thing, the mark of a writer worried about getting their meaning across; equally bad is the fact that, like many descriptors, they're often quite vague. In 99 percent of cases, well-written dialogue and context will work perfectly well without any need of adverbial support: trust your reader to get it. Use adverbial tags if you absolutely must, but only if there's no elegant way around it—and there almost always is.

Third, avoid substitutes for the word *said*. Referred to in the trade as *said-bookisms*, these toxic usages will mark you as a beginner and get you a rejection slip faster than anything, and rightly so. A very short list of these would include

> He/She *sneered, snarled, grunted, growled, grated, uttered, complained, requested*, and of course the infamous, *ejaculated. Hissed* is also out unless the word or sentence contains sibilants ("s" sounds)… you cannot, ever, hiss a sentence like, "Get on with it." Just try it.

New writers typically use these terms because they think readers will get tired of the word *said*. This is wrong: *said* is quite transparent, and should be used in every instance. It's permissible to very occasionally and appropriately use *asked, replied, whispered, muttered, yelled, screamed, replied*. Once in a novel, you might even use *ordered* or *demanded*. But please keep it to that.

Truly unpardonable is the excruciating *swiftie*, a dialogue tag that uses a pun to connect it to the preceding text. An example of this would be

> "The brook is so high it's flooding the meadow," she babbled wetly.

The garrote is too easy a death for writers who do this.

Fourth and final, when you need to tag a longer line of dialogue consisting of several clauses or sentences, do it either before or right after the first words or clause, wherever if fits naturally. Take this:

> "Look love, I'm bloody exhausted. It's not that I don't want to do it, I just haven't got the energy, all right?" said Charles.

See the problem? The reader doesn't know who's speaking till the end. The solution of course is to recast it in one of two ways:

> "Look love," said Charles, "I'm bloody exhausted. It's not that I don't want to do it, I just haven't got the energy, all right?"

> Charles said, "Look love, I'm bloody exhausted. It's not that I don't want to do it, I just haven't got the energy, all right?"

That's it for tags. While we're at it, an unrelated but still common sin: when a line of dialogue ends with a question mark, the tag following it does *not* need to be capitalized (see my first example above).

Dialogue Real and Unreal

Unlike some other sections of this book, I don't have much comment on the conventional wisdom and "rules" which apply to dialogue: they are, in the main, sound. I will say though that some writers have a better ear for dialogue than others. We speak of people having a "tin ear", meaning they're insensitive to nuance and shading in either song or speech. Since dialogue is a very dynamic thing, full of rhythm, modulation, idiom, tone, and much more, a writer with a tin ear is going to have trouble writing good dialogue.

The question is whether someone who doesn't naturally have a good ear for dialogue can learn to represent dialogue well on the page. I think it's possible, but it requires two things: the awareness that one's fictional dialogue needs improvement (and that applies to 99 percent of writers, myself included), and the willingness to work at it. There are several ways one can approach this.

The first thing to do is read good fiction. In particular, look for those authors that write really good dialogue. A lot of these are crime writers: Elmore Leonard, Agatha Christie, and Raymond Chandler come to mind at once. Beyond that, Charles Portis, Stephen King, Mary Doria Russell, and Douglas Adams are all masters of the spoken exchange.

It goes without saying that dialogue should flow well. Mark Twain summarized pretty much everything about dialogue in one of his eighteen rules of writing:

> *When the personages of a tale deal in conversation, the talk shall sound like human talk, and be talk such as human beings would be likely to talk in the given circumstances, and have a discoverable meaning, also a discoverable purpose, and a show of relevancy, and remain in the neighborhood of the subject in hand, and be interesting to the reader, and help out the tale, and stop when the people cannot think of anything more to say.*

When it comes to talk sounding like human talk, I have to say that when editing or critiquing newer writers' manuscripts, I often find myself tempted to drink well before cocktail hour by their frequent and maddening failure to use contractions. I don't care what you were taught by your high school English teacher: in the real world, people—including the most highly-educated—use contractions *all the time*.

Imagine reading the following line of dialogue in a book:

> "I will not do it. I do not care whether you are going to pull that trigger or not, I am not going to do that."

This is how evil overlords and arrogant nobles speak; the Sheriff of Nottingham, perhaps. If a character in a story uses this sort of stiff, formal speech, any sane reader is going to, at minimum, dislike the character at once for their pomposity; they're equally likely to dislike the author, and put the book down for good. It's *painful*, people!

Similarly, it's perfectly all right to use contractions in narrative, and certainly in interiority. A failure to use contractions where most native English speakers would draws the wrong kind of attention to the writing in a scratchy, stiff-collared sort of way.

So listen to the language spoken around you, read good writers, and try to develop an ear for dialogue and the natural flow of spoken exchanges. If you don't have a natural ear—and most of us don't—it's going to take time and work to get your dialogue to flow. But persistence and applied intelligence will get you there.

Subtext

It's also important to note that people often don't say what they mean. When, for example, your characters are trying to avoid touching on a sensitive topic that nonetheless needs addressing—the proverbial elephant in the room—they'll often make small talk or dance around the topic, talking about anything but the thing that matters; but any listener or reader with active grey cells will see right through the avoidance strategy to the unspoken thoughts, feelings, and conflict the speakers are avoiding.

This sort of unspoken content in a verbal exchange is called *subtext*, and when used correctly it's extremely powerful. It's the real message under the (often bland) surface of the dialogue.

One of the most memorable examples of subtext ever written comes from the terrific 1944 film noir, *Double Indemnity*. A sharp, handsome salesman, Walter Neff (Fred MacMurray) visits a client's home to discuss his insurance policy. The man is out, and Neff begins talking to the client's lovely wife Phyllis Dietrichson (Barbara Stanwyck). After a little preamble, Neff suddenly switches from the topic of insurance to a personal question:

NEFF
I wish you'd tell me what's engraved on that anklet.

PHYLLIS
Just my name.

NEFF
As for instance?

PHYLLIS
Phyllis.

NEFF
Phyllis. I think I like that.

PHYLLIS

But you're not sure?

NEFF

I'd have to drive it around the block a couple of times.

Neff has made it clear that he's interested in her, and she gives the impression ("But you're not sure?") that she doesn't resent this interest. In reply, Neff is saying that he'd like the opportunity to get to know her. At this point, Phyllis stands up, indicating their conversation is over. She's wonderfully ambiguous here, playing the proper wife yet testing him to see if he'll go further as the dialogue continues.

PHYLLIS

Mr. Neff, why don't you drop by tomorrow evening about eight-thirty. He'll be in then.

NEFF

Who?

PHYLLIS

My husband. You were anxious to talk to him weren't you?

NEFF

Sure, only I'm getting over it a little. If you know what I mean.

PHYLLIS

There's a speed limit in this state, Mr. Neff. Forty-five miles an hour.

NEFF

How fast was I going, officer?

PHYLLIS

I'd say about ninety.

By now, without a word being spoken about attraction or desire, the audience is in no doubt as to what's really going on. Neff is hooked, and the sexual tension is palpable. Neff decides to raise her, (to use a poker metaphor), upping the stakes:

NEFF

Suppose you get down off your motorcycle and give me a ticket.

PHYLLIS

Suppose I let you off with a warning this time.

NEFF

Suppose it doesn't take.

PHYLLIS

Suppose I have to whack you over the knuckles.

NEFF

Suppose I bust out crying and put my head on your shoulder.

PHYLLIS

Suppose you try putting it on my husband's shoulder.

NEFF

That tears it.

Phyllis matches the stakes and raises them again, toying with him to see how far he'll go. Finally, she sees his hand by mentioning her husband. Neff folds, picks up his hat and briefcase, and becomes the professional insurance salesman again.

NEFF

Eight-thirty tomorrow evening then, Mrs. Dietrichson.

PHYLLIS
That's what I suggested.

He leaves, but of course what's been said can't be unsaid. It's clear to everyone that these two are going to take this further.

Voice

Character voice and narrative voice are critical to the point of being under-valued in their importance. When the author's control over voice falls short, the result is that a good story at best fails to meet its potential and at worst doesn't engage the reader enough to keep them reading. Voice conveys the personality and mood of the character telling the story, and has an effect on the reader's perception of events.

In life, one of the reasons we find some people interesting and others dull is their voice. So what is this mysterious voice thing? For the writer, voice is many things: the way a person expresses themselves through speech, their word choices, speech rhythms, sentence structure, and level of diction: in the real world, add in voice pitch and timbre, and, in some cases, accent.

But voice goes much deeper than that, especially in interiority, where we're not hearing direct, spoken speech but instead *free indirect discourse* (much more on this later), the character's thoughts as they occur in their head. This is where character voice is at its most important. With the author guiding (enticing? Seducing?) them, the reader gets to look at the story world and the events taking place therein from behind the character's eyes, revealing the character in a profound, experiential way; we are shown not only what the character thinks but *how* they think it. Voice in interiority can be an extremely powerful device in shaping a reader's understanding of and insight into a character. Take this passage from Loreth Anne White's powerful ro-mantic suspense novel, *A Dark Lure*:

> *Cole was now ready to draw his battle line in the sand. Whatever in the hell his father did with this ranch, it wasn't going to Forbes, not on his watch. It was the principle of the thing. Before, Cole didn't care. Now he did. This ranch fell under the Agricultural Land Reserve. By law it had to be used for farming. It couldn't be developed without government maneuvering. And he suddenly couldn't bear the thought of it being sliced and sold off in pieces.*

Maybe it was his own long-held animosity toward Forbes. Or maybe it was Olivia. He didn't the hell know, but the fire was back in him. And he liked the feel.

We see the effect of voice at its most powerful with jokes. Given a good joke to tell, some will pull it off better than others: that's the result of voice (with, admittedly, a side serving of comic timing). A good voice will engage and hold the reader, and if that voice is telling an interesting story, the writer's work has suddenly become much easier.

An important point to make is that in a book with multiple viewpoint characters, the viewpoint's narrative or interior voice should align to some degree with the character's direct voice. I say *to some degree* because while your characters' direct (i.e., dialogue or spoken) voices might vary enormously, their internal or indirect voices when we're in their thoughts generally shouldn't exactly mirror their direct voice.

Imagine a scene where you have an uneducated PoV character (let's call him Tom) with a vocabulary of just a few hundred words speaking in dialect: their dialogue might sound something like,

"How you expect me to know that? I don't know nothin. I warn't never there. That sumbitch Rick's full of it, a lyin sack of shit. I'm outta here."

In this dialogue, I've purposely, for voice, omitted two terminal *G*s as well as the apostrophe usually used to mark them; I've left out a verb ("do" should have been the second word); and used three informal contractions ("warn't," "sumbitch," and "outta").

When you switch to their internalization or free indirect speech, you'll want to keep the feeling of the character's voice. So in this instance, the interiority following the dialogue above might read,

He took off right there, wasn't going to hang around for the cops to come and cuff him. Sure Rick was lying, but after what went down, they weren't going to take his word over Rick's, no sir.

Note that the level of diction and syntax are somewhat aligned to the character's speaking voice, but I've maintained standard correct grammar and spellings throughout.

Now let's look at how these lines might have been written if Tom were a college-educated character:

"How would I know that? I don't know anything. I wasn't even there. Rick's lying to you, he's always been full of it. I'm out of here."

He ran, wasn't going to wait for the police to come and arrest him. Of course Rick was lying, but after what happened, they weren't going to take his word over Tom's, not for a moment.

The difference between a so-so voice and a polished one can make or break the best story. Especially in the opening scenes.

Openings

It's impossible to overstress the importance of a story's opening. With on-line bookstores offering "look inside" previews, the first few paragraphs—even the first paragraph alone—are likely to be the deciding factor between someone buying the book or moving on. Ditto with a slush reader, agent, or editor—in fact, more so. If those first lines aren't doing exactly what they should, the reader will simply think, *not for me*, and move on to the next potential purchase.

The good news is that openings are actually easy: all an author has to do is keep the person reading. That's all there is to it. Of course, good prose helps—those early paragraphs need to be your best writing, free of typos or infelicities of grammar and syntax. But let's assume you know how to do that.

For an opening to work, the writer needs to quickly do four things: (1) show something happening; (2) make the reader care about the outcome; (3) provide enough specific detail (description) so that the picture comes into sharp focus; and (4) convince the reader that the writer knows what he or she is about, and that the reader's time will be rewarded if they just keep reading. At the same time, a good writer will also be laying the foundations of scene, setting, and character.

Having something happening doesn't mean you have to have slam-bang action from the first sentence—in fact, supplying wild action without giving the reader a reason to care is often a guaranteed fail, especially in the hands of young males writing fantasy. Like so much writing dogma, the advice to *begin with action* is terribly prone to misunderstanding. What's needed is to raise a question in the reader's mind and quickly follow up with a reason to care. If a story begins,

Jim Conroy sat in the center of the tiny cabin, his worldly belongings arranged neatly on the bone-dry floorboards. A ritual invocation, perhaps, of a lost order.[9]

---

9   Taken from my own short story, "Appalachian Fall".

this immediately raises a number of questions. Although the reader has no reason yet to care who Jim Conroy is, his action—arranging his worldly belongings neatly before him, and the hint that this is somehow connected to something vanished (a "lost order")—suggests that something is going on, that he's doing this for a purpose; this is likely to pique the reader's interest enough to make them start the next paragraph:

> A tattered old wallet: the slots which had once held platinum and titanium cards sagged empty, and three one-dollar bills occupied the equally dilated billfold area.

This tells the reader that Conroy was once well-off but has stumbled on hard times. And as a person of at least average humanity, the reader will by now probably be starting to feel a little sorry for this guy, because, let's face it, we all fear destitution. But what's the guy doing in this tiny cabin, contemplating his belongings, and why? Is he going to kill himself? Jeez. Let's read on.

> His New York driver's license mocked him from behind a dirty plastic window; the evaporation of his belief in the consensus that made driving possible had been one of the first, and certainly the most sudden, symptoms of his ruin. The inexplicable corruption of his reading and writing skills had followed shortly after.

Okay, now we know there's something really weird going on. This Jim Conroy, whoever he is, is obviously in deep trouble, and an empty wallet may be the least of it. There's a strong suggestion of mental illness, but the cumulative effect of the words *ritual*, *ruin*, and *corruption*, suggest something darker, more eldritch at work. The reader wants more…

Although Conroy is simply sitting contemplating his belongings and there is no overt action, the opening is *character in action*—a character is *doing* something, something interesting, and the reader is hooked.

The opening hook, therefore, needn't be in-your-face drama. Anything that stirs the reader's curiosity can work. Sometimes just a strong or unique enough narrative voice will do the trick. Take a powerful narrative voice and combine that with a couple of well-chosen question seeds, and you can craft a very compelling opening, such as the following from Roger Zelazny's 1969 novel, *Isle of the Dead*:

> Life is a thing—if you'll excuse a quick dab of philosophy before you know what kind of picture I'm painting—that reminds me quite a bit of the beaches around Tokyo Bay.
>
> Now, it's been centuries since I saw that Bay and those beaches, so

*I could be off quite a bit. But I'm told that it hasn't changed much,
except for the condoms, from the way that I remember it.*

There follow two pages—*two pages!*—of descriptive reminiscence and philosophizing in which Zelazny slowly reinforces his metaphor, eventually tying it up with the narrator's present predicament. This strategy of hijacking the reader at the get-go and taking them on a detour via two pages of descriptive matter after just two introductory paragraphs is a bold one, and it succeeds brilliantly.

Why does it work? Because in those two brief, introductory paras, Zelazny has both hit you with a first-person narrative voice as confident as any Greek tragedist and planted a couple of hooks so powerful (a centuries-old narrator, and the sly but purposeful mention of condoms) that you'll almost certainly stick around to hear him out.

A reader's attention is a fragile thing in the first several pages of a story; once further into the book, by which time you'll have hopefully convinced them that you know where you're going and have the skills to make the trip worthwhile, the reader is less easily thrown and will cut you more slack for digression, picture-painting, windy philosophizing, and the like: but at the beginning, your job is simply to snag the reader's attention and lead them unresisting into your world.

At the same time, in the interest of helping the reader get oriented and smoothing their entry into the story, it helps to address all, or at least most, of what are commonly termed the "five journalistic questions"—*who, what, where, how, and why*—in the first scene.

In summary, then, your opening should do these things:

- Raise a question

- Make the reader care

- Begin to flesh out character

- Make the setting real in the reader's mind and provide an anchor for the scene

- Answer the five journalistic questions (who, what, when, where, and why)

Prologues

Another piece of widespread dogma is the notion that prologues are some-how wrong and outmoded and certain to kill your novel. This is faddish twaddle started by agents and editors who—by virtue of reading so much slush—see a lot of terrible fiction with awful prologues. As John Gardner put it, "One should fight like the devil the temptation to think well of edi-tors.... By the nature of their profession they read too much, with the result they grow jaded and cannot recognize talent though it dances in front of their eyes."

Readers, the ones who actually pay money to buy the book, supporting the entire industry in the process, have no problem at all with a *well-written and interesting* prologue.

If your story needs a prologue to set the scene or tone, to introduce the theme or to impart some critical backstory or information upfront, use one. Just be sure it's relevant, interesting, and as brief as you can make it. Apply the things I told you about openings just above, and keep it as tight as you can.

Interiority

What then, is interiority, aka *internal dialogue, internalization,* or, more for-mally, *free indirect discourse or free indirect speech*? The definition in *Wikipe-dia* is nicely concise on this:

Free indirect speech is a style of third-person narration which uses some of the characteristics of third-person along with the essence of first-person direct speech.[10]

A Note on Filtering

True free indirect speech is different to *filtered* thought and feeling in that it penetrates deeper into viewpoint. Accordingly, when critiquing or mentoring others, I always advise them against *filtering*. Filtering is when the character's thoughts and feelings (which, unlike actions, happen on the inside) are mediated, or *told* by the author. These occurrences are always flagged by

---

10   From Wikipedia again: According to British philologist Roy Pascal, Goethe and Jane Austen were the first novelists to use this style consistently[,] and nineteenth century French novelist Flaubert was the first to be consciously aware of it as a style.

filtering words, verbs such as *thought, felt, realize, watch, look, could, decide, seemed, assumed,* etc.[11] Filtering words are often accompanied by supporting adjectives.

My advice is to eliminate these ruthlessly and instead go for full interiority in every case. Go visceral. Except for those brief times you really need to impart a lot of information that wouldn't be flowing through the character's head, put your reader in the character's skin and *keep them there.*

Here's the difference in action (filtering in bold):

Filtered speech:

> She slammed her door and fell into the chair, **thinking** how badly she'd let him down. She **told herself** she should been there for him. She **knew she** could never face him again.

Free indirect speech (aka interiority):

> She slammed her door and fell into the chair. God, she'd let him down so badly. She should have been there for him. She'd never be able to face him again

Before we dig deeper into this, let me just state that although some writers still use italics for directly represented thoughts, it's really not necessary and, to some extent, reminds us we're reading a story. For instance, here's the sentence above using directly represented thoughts ("I" instead of "she"), and shown first with, then without italics:

> She slammed her door and fell into the chair. *God, I let him down so badly. I should have been there for him. I'll never be able to face him again.*

> She slammed her door and fell into the chair. God, I let him down so badly. I should have been there for him. I'll never be able to face him again.

See what I mean? Not only no filtering, but direct with no italics. And yet, you understood that the first-person bits represent the character's direct thought in their own head, right? Just be clear in your own mind what is gesture, what is interiority, and what is direct thought, and all will be well.

⊘

---

11   I've given these verb examples in the past tense, but obviously they will appear in whatever tense the story is written in. Nor is filtering limited to interiority—it can be found in narration, too, and is usually best cut out.

Narrative Distance

When you delve into writing manuals, you'll see discussions of *narrative distance*. The standard metaphor used to describe this is that of a movie camera: as the narrative distance decreases, as it does in the examples above, the effect is one of slipping from an outside view of the character into their head. The camera (which is the reader's impression of how close they are to the PoV character's viewpoint) seems to zoom in as narrative distance shrinks: the reader ceases to be an external observer and, when technique is well-handled, slips into the character's skin, seeing through their eyes, feeling their feelings, sensing what the character senses.

But who's holding the camera? (Cue old Monty Python *Who's Filming Us Now* sketch and the dizzying concept of infinite regression.) Seriously, though…

It's worth reminding ourselves that the author is the one behind *everything* that takes place on the page, though it doesn't appear that way. In any story, a number of people, both real and fictional, collaborate to make the story work. These include:

1. The real author

2. The fictional author (author speaking in narrative voice)

3. The fictional characters

- (speaking in narrative)

- (speaking in interiority)

- (speaking in direct speech)

4. The reader

Returning then to narrative distance (and this has a lot to do with viewpoint), if the object is to pull the reader deeply into the fictional dream and make them align with the protagonist so that they care deeply about the outcome, why would one ever pull the camera back, keeping the narrative cool and objective?

The most appropriate time to do this is at the opening of a novel, perhaps the opening of a chapter or scene, and pretty much *nowhere else*. In these cases, you might even want to have an external narrator (the fictional author), setting the stage in the traditional manner more or less unchanged from the days of the Greek tragedists.

But the most powerful stories are usually best told by the characters themselves, whether in narrative, interiority, or dialogue. Everything is seen through the eyes of the characters, everything told through their voice—yes, I did say *told*, and I'll elaborate on that later. Though arguments can be mounted for moving that camera back and forth on the dolly, all the time changing narrative distance, I contend that this is advice based largely on the historic evolution of literary style and the conventions of film—which last, incidentally, are to this author's view doing a lot to transform and even ruin the novel.

Quite often it'll *feel* as though there's an external narrator at the beginning of a scene, giving an overview and generally setting the stage and imparting necessary information in the first sentences. But within a few paragraphs at most, if the author is skilled, a seamless hand-off takes place and it becomes clear that we're in one of the character's heads, hearing their voice.

In essence, there's no real need, in most third-person PoV fiction, for an external narrator. With clever use of voice, even broad and complex information can be transmitted without sacrificing interiority. Take for example the Argentine writer Jorge Luis Borges, one of the towering figures of 20th century literature. Borges's short stories typically examine and feature dizzying metaphysical or philosophical ideas, and he uses a variety of techniques and viewpoints. When Borges uses third-person, he may open a story addressing the reader directly in narrative; but soon his narrative voice as an author blends so smoothly into the viewpoint's narrative voice that once the viewpoint character is introduced, it *feels* as though we were in the viewpoint all along rather than being addressed by the author.

How is this possible? Because the author is *in* the story and not external to it. They are narrating events from the ground, from within, with the judgment and perspective and feelings of a character, not an external narrator and certainly not the author. This is something that all good authors who have mastered their craft do reflexively, and something you should strive for also.

My own preference, and this is the way some of the most successful authors write, is to *never* pull out of the viewpoint's skin. Never go cool. Go from hot to molten in the way your reader is shown the story world and in the interactions of your characters. Why, for goodness's sake, would you want to take them out the characters' skins and remind them that the story they're reading is being told, and made up, by an external author? This isn't the nineteenth century.

Yes, intense interiority is a modernist technique and perhaps a passing fad; I'm generally against fashions in writing, but *as a reader* I find this technique, along with voice, to be a highly effective device for keeping the reader immersed in the story. Although there are many authors who employ external narrators very effectively (Borges is one, John Le Carré is another), it takes a lot of skill to do without introducing a sense of detachment or fumbling the transitions from external narrator to character voice.

One exception to this advice to stay hot and interior might be when the trauma or horror of a scene is so profound that it forces dissociation, and the viewpoint character experiences a complete shutdown of or detachment from their feelings; they become a camera, because the intensity of feeling would be so powerful as to shut down rational thought. This self-protective mechanism of the human psyche is well-documented and can be used to good effect by the author.

Most of the writers I admire don't ever show themselves on the page. *Everything* in a particular scene, even the most trivial details of setting and stage direction, is deeply colored by the viewpoint character, their feelings, their preferences, their prejudices, their state of mind. Everything comes with judgment.

In summary, my advice is to keep the narrative distance tight and not pull the camera back, taking the reader out of your viewpoint character's head, unless you have a very good reason to do so. As with PoV consistency, it's vital that the author remain in full control of narrative distance and viewpoint penetration at all times.

Flashbacks, Flashforwards, and Playing with Time

Contrary to current dogma, flashbacks that are *relevant to the story* do not slow the pacing. Nor is there any reason not to have a flashback in the opening scenes. Like so much other conventional "wisdom", this is anything but. You are God in your fiction, and free to employ any device you wish so long as you have the chops, the *craft*, and the voice to pull it off. The only thing that matters is that the reader stays engaged and enjoys the ride. If they're enjoying the ride, they'll follow wherever you lead them.

Storytelling, like everything, follows trends and fashions. As readers (and viewers, in the case of visual narrative) grow more sophisticated, their ability to follow and even their enjoyment of nonlinear narrative techniques increases. Flashbacks and nonlinear techniques go back as far as the Arabian Nights tale of *Sinbad the Sailor*, and were employed by Emily Brontë in her 1847 classic, *Wuthering Heights*. More recent and wilder examples include Marcel Proust, James Joyce, and of course Kurt Vonnegut's brilliant novel, *Slaughterhouse Five*.

Occasionally, and especially in modern mystery/suspense films, the technique is overused to the point where the reader or viewer spends much of the time lost and disoriented, trying to make sense of the events taking place, unsure what is going on when or even where. I'm sure there's a small percentage of the audience who are impressed by this, but I'm of the opinion that reading should be enjoyable, not hard, frustrating work more concerned with showing off the author's cleverness than giving their audience a worthwhile experience. Where you choose to draw the line is up to you, but do be aware there is one.

A Note on Suspense

The notion that suspense is based on mystery and keeping things from the reader is generally wrong. Suspense is achieved by foreshadowing and even plainly stating that Bad Things are going to happen to a character for whom the reader cares without necessarily telling them *when* or *how*. In general, foreshadowing ought to be subtle, but sometimes you can just come right out and tell the reader. The brilliant and much-lamented Douglas Adams (of *Hitchhiker's Guide to the Galaxy* fame) does exactly that in his novel, *Dirk Gently's Holistic Detective Agency*. He opens Chapter Seven, where he introduces Gordon Way, the female lead's brother, with the line

> *This was the evening of the last day of Gordon Way's life, and he was wondering if the rain would hold off for the weekend.*[12]

Suspense, you see, is about anticipation and foreboding. In my nonfiction book *Aegean Dream*, the tragicomic, bittersweet true story of the year my wife and I lived on a small Greek island, I open Chapter One with a small note right under the chapter head that reads,

> *There are a thousand ways in which a heart can be broken.*
> *This is a true story.*

More foreshadowing and explicit hints follow; and although things don't go sideways till around the halfway point, many readers have told me that

---

12   As well as creating suspense, this is an example of mastery of viewpoint. Adams laughs at the rules. That first line is clearly omniscient, but the rest of the scene is told in third person from Way's viewpoint, colored by his judgments and opinions...except where Adams again breaks briefly into omniscient and then into a third party's thoughts. The vast majority of the book is written in third person, but Adams dives into omniscient at will in these instances and it *totally* works. Drown the cat!

although they knew things were going to go very wrong, they kept turning pages, hoping against hope that somehow it would work out okay.

This is why it's critical, as we discussed in the Character chapter, to make your reader care about the protagonist(s). If you achieve that, any suspicion that ugly things are going to happen to them creates suspense and tension in the reader.

Endings

Endings are difficult.

One of the problems the author faces is that different readers will have different expectations as well as a different notion of what is fair. The more complex and better-written the story, the more chance there is that some readers will come away feeling either partly or wholly frustrated.

One very notable example of this is Stephen King's masterpiece, *The Stand*. Many readers claim King uses a *Deus ex machina* to drive the ending, completely ignoring the fact that the accidental release of a virulent plague which is the book's core premise itself represents an act of God. This is a book about Good vs. Evil, and the hand of God is moving behind the scenes.

As for the ambiguity of the book's closing lines, which drives some authors and editors I know to distraction, I find them perfectly appropriate. Where God may have been working to tip the scales at key points, King ends the book by essentially saying that it's up to us where we go from here now that we have the opportunity to start over. What the heck is the problem here?

Some people, and far too many publishing industry professionals, want endings where everything is tied up in a pretty ribbon, with all the loose ends trimmed and tucked securely into place, and maybe a moral lesson of some kind, too. It seems to be an article of faith in the publishing industry that American readers have a problem with ambiguity and loose ends, and the notion may be rooted in historical fact. But I believe that's changed, and that the reading (and moviegoing) public is actually far more sophisticated than industry professionals give them credit for. It's the same old paternalistic, we-know-what's-best-for-you approach, and it's sad that so many writers desperate to be published just go along with the rules, perpetuating this fallacy to please agents and suits.

That said, it's true that some genre readers, notably romance, have very strong expectations in this area: they want their HEA (Happy Ever After, though this is shifting to HFN [Happy For Now]) ending, and by God, the writer better deliver it. Fair enough.

At the other extreme, we have the curious example of literary fiction, where the happy ending is looked upon with such suspicion that works which appear literary in every regard but end well for the protagonist are frowned upon by critics and the self-important arbiters of literary merit as dangerous excursions from the well-trodden road of misery.

This is yet more nonsense. Sure, life is difficult. Sometimes it's nasty, brutish, and short. But I submit that fiction can be both literary and uplifting, and that in life—which, let's face it, is where reality actually resides—some stories *do* end well. In short, the literary snobs can shove their arguments about realism: realism is not incompatible with a good outcome. Yes, that good outcome may be complicated and nuanced, but there's nothing, *nothing*, inherently wrong with a literary or realist work ending well for the protagonist.

A Hard Trick

The greatest difficulty in crafting a satisfying ending is that it both needs to follow logically from all the story events leading up to it and yet surprise the reader; the ideal ending is both inevitable and yet unexpected. This is a hard trick to pull off.

Typically, in genre fiction, the reader will expect one of two endings: protagonist wins or protagonist loses. The author needs to look for the third ending. This may involve cost or sacrifice, with the protagonist having to make a hard choice or give up something of great value in order to achieve their primary goal. Alternatively, they may lose the big prize but walk away with a consolation prize, which may be as simple as an epiphany.

For some terrific examples of effective endings, I'd again direct the reader to John Le Carré, a master of the big climax and satisfying, resonant resolution. His novels *Smiley's People* and *The Night Manager* showcase some of the best endings in any fiction you'll find. (Interestingly, in the latter novel the ending was a great deal more nuanced and thought-provoking than in the fine 2016 miniseries, which opted for one of the obvious endings; I can only assume the producers thought the audience for the TV series, or perhaps today's audience in general, less sophisticated that the readers of the novel.)

Great authors frequently use recurring images and other devices to punch up their endings. Pacing also plays a major role, enabling the climax of a story to ramp up exponentially and last long enough to be truly satisfying:

a four-hundred-page novel that crests and breaks in just two pages is going to leave the reader feeling cheated.

On the other hand, once the business is done, it's time to turn off the lights and draw the curtain. As the saying goes, *always leave them wanting more.* This isn't at odds with satisfying the reader, but too many writers can't seem to bear to let go even after the story is complete. Once the fat lady has sung, it's over, done, *finis.*

Finally, I believe that the more complexity and texture you have in your story, the greater the available threads to weave that satisfying ending. A great piano sonata will require all seven octaves and eighty-eight keys of the piano keyboard: you're not going to be able to play it as the composer intended on a forty-nine-key home digital piano. I'm not saying you *have* to make your story complicated, but when you're casting about for ways to bring everything to a thunderous climax at the end, it certainly helps to have more resources available to draw upon.

THREE: LARGER CONCERNS

Write to please just one person. If you open a window and make love to the world, so to speak, your story will get pneumonia. — Kurt Vonnegut

Honesty and Truth

When you get into a character's head, you have to do it *honestly*. You have to *mean it*.

What do I mean by honesty here? I mean it's not enough to simply stuff the reader inside a character's head and relate their thoughts, attitudes, and beliefs: the author themself[13] needs to be in there, 100 percent emotionally aligned with their character; and if the author lacks the empathy and passion to do that, the result will feel mechanical and rote rather than visceral and real. If an author isn't fully in touch with their characters, the reader intuitively senses that the characters are puppets and constructs, not living, breathing people. Readers know truth. They know it in their bones.

Take this scene from the opening of Bonnie Randall's fine supernatural romance, *Divinity and the Python,* in which protagonist Shaynie Gavin is tending bar at The Python, Edmonton's hopping-est nightclub:

> *"Typically when the city's pro hockey team played at home their tills sang, but tonight…she glanced around, feeling as dumb as the gaggle of girls who stood wallflower-esque beside the dance floor. All dressed up in the wrong place to go. She almost felt sorry until—*
>
> *"Omigod! Jude!" One, a sky-scraper blonde, deliberately stretched high enough to lift her skirt, flash an electric-hued thong. […] "God bless her with a little self respect," Shaynie muttered, but as Panties the Blonde snake-danced toward her station she pasted on a glittering, please-tip-me smile.*

---

13   I realize this usage will startle some readers, but, it is not incorrect. The alternatives are to use gender-specific pronouns (himself/herself), the awful s/he, the clunky catch-all "himself or herself", or else a gender-neutral third-person plural pronoun for a singular subject (i.e., "the author themselves"), which I will not do in my own book. The use of "themself" as a gender-neutral third-person singular pronoun dates back to the fifteenth century and, although not currently in widespread use, is entirely defensible and upheld by the Oxford University Press…he declared customarily. (See what I did there?)

Notice the heat and intense judgment in there? That's the mark of a writer's honesty and their ability to align fully with their character: the author knows both Shaynie and "Panties" are as real as you or I and, by simple osmosis, the reader cannot help but know it too: disbelief is fully suspended, the fictional dream becomes reality. We've seen people behave exactly like this, and we've thought Shaynie's (the PoV character's) same thoughts. The author has parted the veil, shown us the real, and we have fully slipped into their story world.

Here's another example, this time from William Hertling's superb tech thriller *Kill Process*, between two awkward teens who've just met:

> *I have nothing to do after school and my mom won't return until after five, so I walk home with Sean. He offers me a Marlboro Red, which I accept eagerly. I can't afford to buy my own. He flips a brass Zippo open to light me. We argue about whether Metallica or Slayer is better, and he tells me stories about doing mushrooms with his ex-girlfriend.*
>
> *When we get to his house, he yells that he's home, and we go up to his room without waiting for a response. There's a faint yell of his mother's response, which he ignores. Once in his bedroom, he locks the door. His room is overflowing with dirty clothes, metal posters, and random shit. Other than my cousin's, I've never been in a boy's bedroom before. He sits in front of his computer at a desk.*
>
> *"Grab a seat," he says, gesturing to his messy bed.*

Perfectly observed and as honest as it gets, right down to the grammatically wrong usage *to light me* and the *random shit* comment in the girl's interiority, nailing the teen voice and vernacular in both cases.

The writer should never be afraid to say what they really mean. Editing yourself because you're worried what your writing or characters may reveal about you is a form of cowardice which the sincere writer needs to let go of.

Likewise with the current fad for "sensitivity readers" and trigger warnings, which I believe is a form of timidity the sincere writer should not give in to. The job of the writer is to put down their truth about their world, about their story, about their characters. If this makes a reader uncomfortable, that reader is free to put down the book at any point—nobody's holding a gun to their head. The notion that it's somehow the writer's or publisher's responsibility to swaddle the reader in cotton wool and treat them like a delicate porcelain figurine, however well-intended, is just silly. Art is not supposed to be comfortable, only honest.

Story and Conflict

Story is what occurs when well-drawn characters with believable goals and motivations interact to spark a chain of events. When the interaction is crafted by a skilled writer, the reader or viewer experiences emotion.

We can loosely speak of three main types of story: comedy, tragedy, and everything else, all of which we can call *narrative fiction.*

Comedy is when the dramatic interaction of characters makes you laugh; comic effect is largely achieved, as Aristotle puts it, by dramatizing the ludicrous, and a comedy generally ends well for the protagonist.

Typically, tragedy is when the drama ends badly for them, but of course most narrative fiction will contain tragic passages. In his *Poetics*, Aristotle provides us a detailed explanation and definition of tragedy (my boldface):

> *A perfect tragedy should, as we have seen, be arranged not on the simple but on the complex plan. It should, moreover, imitate actions which excite pity and fear, this being the distinctive mark of tragic imitation. It follows plainly, in the first place, that the change of fortune presented must not be the spectacle of a virtuous man brought from prosperity to adversity: for this moves neither pity nor fear; it merely shocks us. Nor, again, that of a bad man passing from adversity to prosperity: for nothing can be more alien to the spirit of Tragedy; it possesses no single tragic quality; it neither satisfies the moral sense nor calls forth pity or fear. Nor, again, should the downfall of the utter villain be exhibited. A plot of this kind would, doubtless, satisfy the moral sense, but it would inspire neither pity nor fear; for **pity is aroused by unmerited misfortune, fear by the misfortune of a man like ourselves.***

Note how nice a distinction Aristotle gives us: it's not enough to just show us the changes of fortune of a character: for the reader (or viewer, in the case of a dramatic performance) to care, that character must either not deserve the misfortune and/or be someone *like ourselves.*

With regard to the antagonist, I find it interesting that Aristotle mentions that the "utter villain's" downfall would (only) satisfy the moral sense. That's good enough for a start, but we can extrapolate that if we make our villain relatable as well, we stand to walk away with the jackpot by splitting the reader's sympathies.

For a story to work, then, the following basic conditions need to be met:

- The characters must be believable and well-drawn enough for the reader to become invested in them

- The characters must have clashing goals
- The characters must interact as they each pursue their goals

External and Internal Conflict

It's a truth of the human condition that our interest is more easily sparked and our attention held by threats than by good news. We watch the nightly news and read newspapers to keep informed of threats and crises, not to feel warm fuzzies at the good fortune of others—unless they've been snatched, against all odds, from the jaws of death. This focus on negatives and threats is a hardwired survival mechanism from eons past when we weren't at the top of the food chain and lived in constant fear of attack from predators and other small bands of early humans. So it's no surprise that conflict—a condition born of clashing goals between ourselves and others, ourselves and nature, or simply our conflicting inner drives—is a core component of story.

Conflict in story comes from the presence of obstacles between a character and their goal. The conflict can be external or internal. When a rival tries to steal the heart of the woman the hero loves, you have conflict; but the conflict could equally well stem from the fact that geography and life circumstances (distance, children, jobs they can't quit, etc.) keep the couple apart. Going more internal, if the hero's drinking stops him from gaining the affection of the woman he loves, the potential result is the same: hero loses girl. Going deeper still, if the hero's insecurity and lack of self-worth undermines him in his interactions with the object of his affections, he still won't get the girl.

There's a widespread assumption that, since conflict of some sort is an essential component in fiction if we want to have an audience, more must be better. This, like so much else, is a fallacy based entirely on the commercial drivers of the narrative and dramatic arts in the modern world. It's nonsense.

The word *conflict* means serious disagreement or struggle, and we're continually told that for a story to keep the reader hooked you need conflict in every scene, and even every page. This is idiocy. What keeps the reader hooked are questions, often of the will they/won't they kind. Some of these may contain oppositions—a character is hungry but everything conspires to prevent them from eating. Are these conflict? You decide.

Then there's the problem of forced conflict and melodrama.

Take the television series *Downton Abbey*, most of which I enjoy enormously. Despite some superb writing and often brilliant character work (Lady Mary,

Mr. Barrow, et al) this hugely successful series frequently crosses the boundary into soap opera and melodrama. This is of course a subjective judgment; but I contend that though the series is compelling viewing and full of conflict, it often achieves that at the cost of being manipulative. Take for example Mrs. O'Brien, a character entirely lacking in roundness and whose sole purpose is to stir the pot, or consider the repeated and ultimately tedious crises of Mr. Bates's plot arc, and you may see what I mean. The longer the series ran, the further it strayed over the line between natural and forced conflict.

Good conflict needs to be unforced, naturally occurring rather than engineered. The quality and *dimension* of conflict in a given story is important—a hero risking death will command our attention more than a hero risking a few bruises; the protagonist facing ruin engages us more than one facing a parking ticket. But when, as in so many contemporary crime novels and virtually 100 percent of TV and film detective stories, every protagonist comes literally crushed under the weight of internal and external baggage, the effect is inevitably formulaic.

I'm not saying that audiences don't get hooked by this: the runaway success of novels like *The Girl with the Dragon Tattoo* and TV series like *Breaking Bad* speaks for itself. What I *am* saying is that manipulating your audience doesn't equate to good fiction or storytelling. But such is the grip of suits and money on the publishing business that things have become confused.

Each era has its fashions, but the drive in publishing to expand the bottom line has led to a pedal-to-the-metal, all-conflict, all-the-time formula being applied to so much drama that it all starts to look the same. The protagonist was abused as a child, has a deeply dysfunctional family background, custody issues with their ex, struggles with drink, drugs, or both, has endless interpersonal and discipline issues at work, possibly a life-threatening condition…and that's just their backstory.

Sound familiar?

You don't have to cynically manipulate your reader with every tool imaginable to keep them interested. To my mind, the real craftsman strives for economy and originality instead of milking the reader dry by using the exact same template every other novelist and screenwriter out there employs. Yes, some people in real life *do* carry a similar and crushing baggage set, but I submit that to just throw in the kitchen sink because it sometimes works erodes our art and ultimately damages our soul. I'm tempted to use words like "cheap" and "lazy" in regard to this way of overloading a hero with conflict except for the fact that too many writers I respect do this very thing: but I stand by my opinion that the protagonist struggling to even breathe under the load of their internal baggage is a fad born of Hollywood and the ever-intensifying pressure of the bottom line rather than any requirements of story or craft. Was Homer's Ulysses an alcoholic? Was Shakespeare's King Lear abused as a child? While both these things are possible, the power of both these dramatic figures certainly isn't undermined by our not being told.

We are all who we are because of our past, and it's true that our past, and especially deep-rooted childhood experiences and trauma, can predispose us to certain behaviors; but this doesn't mean we have to take it to excess.

Let's take as an example John Le Carré's character George Smiley, one-time head of the British Secret Service. A somewhat introverted, cerebral figure, Smiley is endlessly cuckolded by his wife Anne, who has taken for a lover one of Smiley's colleagues, the suave, worldly Bill Haydon. But that's it. Along with a sense of his growing age and concomitant vague melancholy, that's the sum total of Smiley's personal baggage and, my God! how much more believable and unique a character Smiley is for that. Nor do audiences balk at Smiley's lack of inner demons: the Smiley novels have sold in the millions, been translated into thirty-six languages, and adapted for radio, television, and film.

Another example: Stephen King. Everything King writes is original, different, and (for very large numbers of readers) utterly compelling. King crafts complex and wholly rounded characters, but each is different. They have baggage: some have a lot of it, some less; but each of his characters nonetheless feels fresh and real and unique, as do his plots. And King's books have sold over 300 million copies, ranking alongside Count Leo Tolstoy in sales.

To show that it's entirely possible to have very successful narrative drama without resorting to crushing internal conflict, and that a perfectly normal, well-adjusted protagonist can still be at the core of a compelling and hugely successful story, consider Frodo in Tolkien's *Lord of the Rings*. At the onset of the story, Frodo is a normal, happy, and well-to-do hobbit. Once the truth about the Ring is revealed, it's all downhill, but Frodo doesn't start off conflicted or struggling against inner demons.

Then there's Detective Chief Inspector Barnaby in the hugely successful British TV series, *Midsomer Murders*: Barnaby has a good family life, lives in a lovely village, and is in fine health and good spirits most of the time. Or Elizabeth Bennett in Jane Austen's *Pride and Prejudice*: other than the ordinary, everyday concerns of living with a neurotic mother, a few silly sisters, and a bookish, eccentric father, Elizabeth is a happy, carefree, normal young woman.

Do we care any less for any of these because they're not struggling to even stand under the burden of emotional baggage? Of course not.

To conclude, the writer doesn't have to follow the herd and pander to current cults in storytelling. One can craft powerful, resonant fiction without over-loading every available slot in a character's makeup. Like everything about your story, your characters' backstory is a *choice—your* choice. Not being bound by ludicrous assumptions and conventions frees us up to tell our own story without imposing someone else's tired template on our characters.

Goals and Stakes

Closely tied to conflict is the matter of *goals* and *stakes*.

For genre fiction to work, someone has to want something (goal) and things must stand in their way (conflict). In addition, there needs to be a reward if the something is attained, and a price to pay if it's not: these are the stakes. And just as in a game of poker, the stakes are likely to be raised at critical points. The stakes of your story are that growing pile of hundred-dollar bills that your protagonist is either going to win or lose—and losing would be catastrophic.

Rising stakes can, and probably should, blindside the characters. Especially fun is when the character does something intended to help lessen the con-flict or to help another character, and in the process inadvertently raises the stakes for themselves, making the situation worse.

Stakes come in different flavors, too: what is at stake for your protagonist—the personal stakes—are often different, though related, to the larger stakes of your story. The protagonist may for instance be motivated by a desire to stop something bad happening to themself or their loved ones (personal or immediate stakes), but their success or failure will have much wider conse-quences (the story stakes).

Where you have conflict, it goes without saying there always need to be stakes, a price for a losing outcome. But does every interaction and every scene require there to be stakes? An author whose business is high-octane war porn or a Hollywood screenwriter would undoubtedly answer yes. I would say it depends on your genre, on what your story is getting at, and, more than anything, on your ability as a writer to keep your reader interested in the story.

To Plot (or Not)

I have no idea why, but the plotter vs. pantser issue generates a lot of passion and even rage in writing fora and discussion groups. I don't know why some people have such a strong compulsion to be right, but I can say with certainty that you should write the way that suits *you*, and disregard all advice to the contrary. Ignore those self-important asses who try to tell you their way is the right way. Opinions are one thing, but where the arts are concerned, assuming your way is *the* way is arrogance, plain and simple.

That said, I have some thoughts to offer up that might shed some light on aspects of this divide.

A few years ago I picked up a book by an author whom I'd enjoyed in the past and which I was very much looking forward to reading. It was a big science fiction novel, and the author is one of those rare few who's managed to break out of the narrow confines of the genre and become a mainstream bestseller. His books are filled with wonder, his stories painted on big canvases—all stuff I love, unlike so much of today's science fiction which I find either preachy, tediously homely, or just plain dull.

After enjoying the first few dozen pages, however, I found myself growing uncomfortable. Despite the great setup, fine writing, wonderful worldbuilding, and solid characterization, the story felt as if it was on rails. It was meticulous, too precise. It was too damn *plotted*.

Every writer's M.O. is different. Whatever anybody tells you, there's no right way to write—there's only what works. Some people are plotters; others, myself included, write largely by the seat of their pants (and get called "pantsers"). Still, it's wise to begin a story with at least a rough idea of what you're about.

I speak from hard experience: having more than once written myself into a corner, I now make sure I have a few things down on paper before I embark on a long work such as a novel. These will include a good setup and a rough outline of the first few scenes to serve as a launch ramp; full notes and backstory on my principal characters, including some psychological profiles about their deeper goals and motivations; an understanding of the "flaw in the universe," the core conflict that drives the plot; some vague notion of the development of the story; and an idea of my ending (all of which can, and likely will, change). But I don't even attempt anything resembling a full outline.

In my novel *Sutherland's Rules,* I put these ideas into practice. I thought long and hard about my principal characters, wrote bios and backstory for them;

most important of all, I worked hard at understanding their conscious and subconscious goals and motivations, hopes and fears, and the relationships between the protagonists; I did the same for the antagonists. With this done, I jotted down not an outline but a very loose exoskeleton. And then I turned everyone loose.

To my amazement, what resulted was a complex and very tightly-plotted story as the protagonists, opposed by their antagonists and forced to work within some tight real-world parameters (windows of opportunity, seasonal factors, physical limits of mass and velocity that bear on their scheme), used all their ingenuity and resources to achieve their goals. By taking the time to really breathe life into my characters, they came alive and worked to achieve their ends without any manipulation or heavy-handed effort on my part. The result is something close to a Swiss watch, far more tightly plotted than anything I could have envisioned, and without ever resorting to what Stephen King calls, "the noisy jackhammer of plot:" I'd put my characters into a predicament and watched them work themselves free, chronicling their progress as they went.

When I sent the revised draft out to my beta readers, two authors I respect a great deal made comments worth examining here. One told me he wished he could plot so well—which made me laugh, as all I'd done was set the characters free to act and react, then chased them around with maps, calendars, and finally stopwatches to make sure it was all possible! The second comment about the book was that I did a fine job of not telegraphing my intentions in advance; well, how could I? How was I to know what my characters would get up to from one minute to the next? All I ever do is watch, and write the action down.

Notice I mentioned "plot" above, but *only as a noun*. I don't trust plotting *in the sense of a detailed, premeditated outline of story events*. I believe plot should be spontaneous, a hyperdynamic web of forces that develops organically as the writer's well-thought-out and very real characters set out to win or lose their battle against each other, themselves, or nature as they try to reverse that flaw in the universe which is the story's central conflict. Plot, to me, is a noun which describes a story whose events are linked by causality.

Author C.J. Cherryh has a particularly luminous sentence on plot in her blog: "I think of [plot] not as anything like a sequence of events, but as a webwork of tension-lines between characters and sets of characters. You pull one—and one yank moves several characters. It's not events. It's tensions."

There is a middle ground between plotting and pantsing in which the author maps out scenes yet allows the characters some autonomy and is open to unexpected and unforeseen turns of events. But when I read a book where the author has mechanically and *rigidly* plotted everything out carefully in advance (the generic Big Name tech thriller/war porn authors that turn out several books a year are power users of this technique), I can quite literally feel—or at least imagine—the poor characters struggling to break free, to have autonomy, to do something spontaneous and unpredictable, all the while screaming, "I am not a character, I am a free man!" It's painful. It's *boring*. Now, I don't *know* if this is actually the way is the way these writers work, but their books feel choreographed and mechanical. And that's the kiss of death for me.

If, on the other hand, the author has done their preliminary work well, and has some clue what they're about in terms of craft, their characters will act like real people in a real situation in the real world rather than marionettes on a stage set. Oh, there'll be some tuning required, and characters may need reining in occasionally, but I find that's more a question of keeping control over their time in public view rather than limiting their actions.

The classic example of this is the minor character or walk-on whose main job is to impart some information to another character or catalyze something else. Heaven knows why, but these minor characters are sometimes so interesting or charismatic they try to take over the show. Don't let them: have them do their job, keep them well-drawn and interesting, but don't get carried away and give them whole chapters when they're only required for a scene.

Consider also that when some authors talk of plotting, they're referring to a rather different process than the premeditated, scene-by-scene working out of story events I'm grumbling about. What some writers do is write an initial outline that's effectively a barebones first draft and in which the characters are organically involved as actors, and then expand that more and more; and I think this is where a good deal of misunderstanding arises as to what plot and plotting are: this kind of loose outlining is very different from imposing a rigid choreography on your poor characters from the major set-pieces down to when they're allowed time for a meal or a cup of coffee.

My personal belief is that the time to plot is *after* you've got the first draft down. Even then, plot in its verb form isn't quite the right word—I prefer to think of it as *outlining* after the fact. And the reason for this is that when you have eighty or a hundred thousand words, dozens of chapters over hundreds of pages that have taken you several months or even years to write, you need to get an overview of the whole. At this point, writing a brief summary of what happens in each chapter and scene is something that I find vital to help me see what needs doing in the rewrite.

For myself, I'll carry on as a pantser. The way I look at it is that if I can't trust my characters to act independently, I've probably not done a very good job on them, have I?

How you write, though, is entirely up to you. Just experiment until you find what works, then stick with it.

Subplots

Conventional wisdom holds that a long work—a novel, say—needs one or more subplots to power it and help it along. I'm not convinced: also, good subplots don't always materially affect the outcome of the main plot arc. But they're certainly useful, primarily, for adding interest and texture and, more importantly, illuminating character and avoiding more exposition.

Lord of the Rings, to take a widely-known example, has several complex subplots woven into it. These include the subplot around Saruman and his machinations, the prideful Denethor's relationship with his sons, and of course the love triangle between Eowyn, Arwen, and Aragorn.

Stephen King's *Misery*, on the other hand, has no subplots at all. It's a straight-ahead story of a writer trying to escape from a crazed serial killer. So it's quite possible for a good writer to write a bestselling 350-page thriller without the need to buttress the main plot with subplots.

One problem with subplots is that they very easily fall into tropes. The worst of these is the dreaded divorced-couple-brought-together-by-crisis trope so beloved of Hollywood action movies, and not a few bestselling novelists either. Please, don't even think of doing this: it was already tired two decades ago. A good subplot should make the outcome of the main plot less predictable, not more so.

It's true that many well-used tropes like the one quoted above, or a protagonist's ongoing struggle with addiction and substance abuse, are effective precisely because they are so very common in real life that large numbers of people can identify with them. That doesn't make them any less contemptible as devices when they're used by default by lazy writers: they're the textese of the plot world, *u kwim?nntr*[14] *LOL*. As I mentioned in the section on story, the very first ideas we get are usually the most tired and recycled, and are best ditched without a second look.

---

14   Text message speak for *you know what I mean?No need to reply.*

The other danger with subplots is that they can cause your story to fork, diluting the energy of the main plot and distracting the author and, consequently, the reader. Like those secondary characters who try to steal the show, subplots need to be kept under tight control and used to add spice and shed light on the main characters and the core conflict. They're called *sub*plots for a reason: these are secondary storylines, and need to be kept that way.

A good subplot will have tension and conflict and stakes all of its own; properly handled, a subplot will weave itself into the main plot arc and materially add to work, bringing depth and color to a story that otherwise might have seemed a little shallow and monochromatic.

Subplots can also be used to distract the protagonist's attention from the core conflict at critical junctures, making them miss opportunities or leading to them deeper into the mess they were already in and raising the stakes in the main plot.

In summary then, by all means set up some subplots in a long work, but remember to keep them under tight control, to *own* them, and to make sure they resolve rather than flapping around at the end of the story…unless you're going to use the subplot to set up the next book in a series.

Pacing

Pacing is the speed at which your story moves, as well as the variations within that. Tension, conflict, and characters' physical actions all affect pacing. There are reams of material written on the topic (entire books, for God's sake, and with diagrams!) but pacing is largely a matter of common sense and intuition. There are a few general remarks which can be made, though.

To begin with, *don't* begin a story at the beginning. Even writers with some experience need to be reminded of this sometimes. Begin (assuming you're writing in something approaching a linear time sequence) when something immediately relevant to the story's core conceit is happening. As I said in the chapter on openings, raise questions and engage the reader's interest to get the story moving. Don't, just don't, start by telling us all about the protagonist and giving us reams of backstory unless you really know what you're doing. And the author who begins with a physical description of the protagonist has probably lost me as a reader already.

Also consider the span of time in which the story, novel, or whatever takes place. A whole novel that takes place within a day (e.g., Dan Brown's *The Da Vinci Code*, or Dean Koontz's *Dragon Tears*) can't help but have faster pacing than a novel that sprawls over months or years. This effect—a lot of events happening in a brief time—is termed *compression*.

Try to avoid concerning yourself too much with pacing in your first draft. For the vast majority of writers, especially those who don't plot in detail, the first draft is where you're working out ideas, trying things out, summarizing in narrative scenes or events which may later be dramatized, etc. Pacing needn't be too much of a concern at this point: although you should try to establish a building momentum, don't fret over this in your first draft. Revision is the time to look hard at your pacing and make sure it's working.

Remember too that pacing happens at every level: the overall pacing of the novel, the pacing of each chapter, the pacing of each scene within those chapters. When you're locked into the minutiae of revision, you'll see pacing at the paragraph and even the sentence level. Take a good thriller or suspense novel written by a master like Stephen King or John Le Carré, and pay attention to how they vary the internal structure of the novel at every level, right down to the quickening sentences at the climax points, so very like the breath coming faster and shorter as you break into a panicked run. Like this brief passage from Stephen King's wonderful 2002 novel, *From a Buick Eight*:

> *He found the doorjamb and gripped. Behind us there was another monstrous purple flash from the Buick, and I could feel the pull of the thing ratchet up another notch. It was like some hideous new gravity. The rope around my chest had turned into a steel band and I couldn't get a single inch of fresh breath. I could feel my eyes bulging and my teeth throbbing in their gums. My guts felt all in a plug at the base of my throat. The pulse was filling up my brain, burning out all conscious thought.*

A few more thoughts to conclude:

- Get rid of scenes that don't in some way advance plot or subplots

- In a genre book, there should be a sense of quickening movement. My personal belief is that a good novel should become hard to put down by the halfway point, and impossible at the two-thirds mark.

- It doesn't hurt to add a "ticking clock"—a time or day, preferably close to the narrative time, when Very Bad Things will happen if the protagonist doesn't achieve their goal, defeat the antagonist, etc.

- If your premise, setup, conflict, and characters are all working well, pacing will take care of itself.

- Trust your intuition and your beta readers

Information Management

A well-told story will engage the reader's curiosity and raise an endless series of questions about the story's characters and their world. The writer needs to anticipate these questions and begin to trickle in the answers (without overloading the reader with backstory or facts) as soon as the need is generated, and certainly before the reader begins to feel impatient at the lack of timely information. The best authors do this invisibly, reflexively; the skill is one that takes some time and effort to master.

The more different the story setting or cultural context, the more information will need to be transmitted to the reader. Nowhere is this harder than in the field of science fiction and fantasy, since authors in these genres have to orient and inform the reader about what may be a drastically different setting or society without bringing the story to a screeching halt.

The crime and mystery writer of course faces a variation of this problem with the need to plant clues and foreshadow events, etc., with just the right degree of dexterity so they don't become obvious to the reader but are there in plain sight nonetheless.

Even when the story world is the everyday one we all inhabit and there are no mysteries to be hidden for armchair sleuths to uncover, there are still plenty of things the reader needs to be told. Characters' backstory, events in the past, facts our characters know, skills they excel at, and so on.

Information is usually best sprinkled in in bite-size pieces; good authors learn to lace it into the story as one might mix a crushed-up pill into a cat's food rather than risk a confrontation by trying to force it down the throat whole. The days when you could get away with massive narrative infodumps like the infamous cetology lecture in *Moby Dick* are long past. Few readers today will put up with three paragraphs of exposition, never mind an entire chapter[15]. The handling of backstory and exposition remains one of the single hardest things that newer writers struggle to address. Faced with the

---

15   This said, I stand by my earlier comments about voice: a good enough author can keep a reader interested pretty much at will.

difficulty of sneaking in information, we're tempted to just throw up our hands and dump it in, hoping the reader will swallow it whole.

There are times when this—an honest, undisguised infodump—is actually the best and most expedient solution to the issue of information management. Literature isn't play- or screenwriting. The ability to use narrative voice and interiority allows us to fill in the spaces between dialogue less obtrusively. This is one reason we *have* narration and interiority, and it's perfectly allowable to deliver needed information without having to dramatize it all if narrative is more natural and/or efficient .[16] The trick is in selecting which information to convey in narrative and how to go about it.

Let me repeat this: sometimes delivering a chunk of exposition without trying to conceal or disguise or break it up is allowable if done well. If—as per the Roger Zelazny example in the chapter on openings—the narrative voice is strong and compelling, the reader won't flinch or balk at even a large chunk of exposition. But it *is* critical to get the timing right, and to be certain the reader either needs or will welcome the information.

In truth, they may not. Much of the backstory (and/or research) work you've done may well be neither necessary nor interesting to the reader: don't force it on them just because you've put work into it. I may love the new granite on my kitchen countertops, but not care in the slightest how it's quarried or imported into the U.S.

The opposite problem to overloading the reader with backstory and information (and this problem crops up with equal frequency) is a lack of timely information, or indeed *any* required information. This inevitably results in the reader becoming confused, frustrated, or both, and just closing the book. The great science fiction writer, editor, and teacher Algys Budrys once said that there are three reader reactions which the writer should always seek to avoid, since any one of them is likely to throw the reader out of the story and make them stop reading. They are:

- "So what?" (the reader doesn't care)

- "Oh yeah?" (the reader doesn't believe it)

- "Huh?" (the reader doesn't get it)

A failure to supply timely information on issues important to the reader's understanding of either the story or the characters, their motivations, etc., is most likely to elicit the last of these, the "Huh?" reflex, as a result of which the reader might well put the book down, perhaps for good.

---

16   As we'll see in the next chapter, "Show, Don't Tell."

The edge which separates these two tendencies—too much information vs. too little—is razor-thin. Most writers will fall on one side or the other. Part of the issue of course is that the writer is too close to the work, and information management is one area in which first readers, beta readers, and critique groups (more on these later) can be most helpful.

Professional authors sooner or later develop a fine intuitive sense about when and how best to deliver needed information and backstory. At its best, this can seem like magic, as though the author has seen into the reader's mind, delivering the information just as the reader realizes they want or need it.

Besides practice, this skill can also be learned by analyzing how other authors do it. Here's a useful trick recommended by CJ Cherryh:

> [Fritz Leiber] was just very, very good at his craft, and slipped information in so deftly you didn't know he'd done it to you. When I was trying to improve my writing I took one of his longest stories and simply marked and mapped how he set up his information. I applied what I learned and sold the very next thing I sent out.

Show, Don't Tell

The *show, don't tell* dichotomy is entirely false: *all* fiction is telling; if it weren't, it would be called story*showing*. The author is telling you a story, and you, the reader, agree to either play along or not. And given that you're paying for the privilege, it had better be well-told.

The nonsense spoken on this subject is legion, with the result that writers drive themselves mad, often wasting days of their time trying to dramatize, in onstage action and dialogue, scenes that could be far more effectively and economically handled another way.

Remember when we talked about narrative distance in the interiority chapter, and I pretty much said, "screw pulling back the camera, keep the narrative distance tight"? Well, strong interiority will feel most like *showing* to the reader, and pulling back so that the reader's not tight in the PoV character's head anymore will feel more like *telling*.

When you read, as any editor does, a lot of newer writers' novels, you'll find they're often puffy, too long by thousands, and sometimes tens of thousands of words, with stiff, awkward scenes that stand out in contrast to the faster, free-flowing sections. One major reason for this is that the poor author has had the tyrannical *Show, Don't Tell* dictum pounded into their brain by so many writing books and blogs and fellow authors that they're terrified to summarize in narrative things which don't need to be dramatized. So they go ahead and build a "live" scene around every particle of information or setting they think the reader may require.

The result of this perceived need to dramatize everything can result, among other things, in pointless scenes where characters talk about things for no reason other than to avoid a narrative passage. The scene isn't doing anything else, and the characters who were so alive earlier have turned strangely wooden. At its worst, you have the dreaded "As you know, Bob" dialogue, a scene in which characters tell one another things they already ought to know.

Don't do this. Ditch these scenes mercilessly.

In my novel, *Sutherland's Rules*, there's a scene in which two of my protagonists have arrived in Afghanistan and spend a day sightseeing in the northern town of Mazar-i-Sharif prior to being taken to a remote farm where important things happen. I'd done a lot of research on the country and the culture, but there was absolutely no reason I could see to dramatize—to *show*, as most people would think—the main part of that day. They're sightseeing, for God's sakes, just acclimating before the real business happens. Here's how I dealt with it:

> *The day was positively magical. Leaving their shoes at the entrance, they toured the grounds of the Blue Mosque, ate naan and spicy kebabs bought from street vendors, and wandered the market. The 'birds' Billy had casually referred to turned out to be white doves, hundreds of them, which clustered at one part of the Blue Mosque like ordinary pigeons did in London's Trafalgar Square or Venice's Saint Mark's. Afghans seemed to have a fascination, almost a fetish for them: was there a symbolism there, something to do with peace, or freedom? There was definitely a bird fixation in the market, too, with rows of vendors who sold nothing but birdcages, ranging from the small and simple to the fantastically ornate. And despite the occasional checkpoint and very visible security in the form of armed men, uniformed and otherwise, people appeared generally relaxed.*

There, now—that didn't hurt a bit, did it? No need for dialogue or having it all happen onstage, you'd have been bored to distraction. Narrative summary in viewpoint works just fine.

I'll say it once again. The *show, don't tell* dichotomy is entirely false: *all* fiction is telling.

Tone

The *tone* of a piece of writing is best described as the overall feel or attitude it conveys about the characters and events in the story. As such, tone can change at any point in a narrative; but, like narrative distance, it needs to always be under the writer's conscious control. Tone is used to underscore and confirm the events of the story through the viewpoint character's emotional reaction to them; because of this, tone is strongly connected to voice and interiority.

Tone can be formal or informal, comic or tragic, loving or aggressive, arrogant or respectful, and much more. Consider the difference between a best man's speech about his friend delivered at a wedding and a eulogy delivered at that same person's funeral: the content may be quite similar, but the tone is likely to be drastically different.

The reason it's so important for the writer to be both aware and in control of tone is that the reader's thoughts and feelings as they read will be guided in part by the author's use of tone. Tone provides a steady, if sometimes subtle, signal to the reader about how they should feel about the story and its cast of characters.

Problems arise when the writer loses control of tone. Since writers are human, this can happen from one scene to the next. If, in the process of reading a scene you've written, you get the feeling there's something off, check to see if there's a tone slip or shift, or perhaps no clear tone at all. Since tone indicates and confirms the viewpoint character's feelings about other characters, story events, etc., a lack of clarity or slip of control on the author's part will leave the reader unsure how to feel about a scene.

Tone matters in every kind of writing, both fiction and nonfiction. It matters in this very book you're reading, and the author should put a lot of thought into the question of tone at both the chapter and overall level. Generally, in a nonfiction piece, whether a simple essay, article, or book-length work, the tone will be consistent from start to finish. In fiction, tone can vary a good deal within the same story.

In a long work such as a novel, there will be a hierarchy or levels of tone. First is the overall tone of the whole; second is the tone of individual scenes and events; and third is the tone inherent in each character's viewpoint.

Tolkien's *Lord of the Rings* gives us some wonderful illustrations of tone in action. The overall tone of the work can be described as epic, mythic, even literary. The early scenes set in the Shire are light, almost fluffy in tone, as are the younger hobbits' (Merry and Pippin's) scenes; The scenes featuring the

Elves tend to the elegiac, to nostalgia and the passing glories of the world; the scenes set in Gondor and Rohan have an aura of the grave and weighty; and the tone of the sections in Moria, or when Frodo and Sam approach and enter Mordor, is positively fraught and dire. As the book progresses, there is a clear change in tone from light-hearted, to serious, to apocalyptic…and finally back to tranquility in a changed world.

Theme

One of the main things that makes a book resonate with the reader is *theme*. Often universal in nature, theme is fundamental, the underpinning of a work.

Earlier on, I defined the story of *The Lord of the Rings* as "the tale of a simple hobbit whose quiet life is overturned when he finds himself the keeper of the One Ring, an artifact of immense power, and the ensuing quest to destroy it." By contrast, the main *theme* of LotR is simply the conflict between good and evil (there are sub-themes, such as the arrogance and temptations of power, the power of humility, courage in the face of certain defeat, and more).

Let's look at some others. In *Star Wars*, the primary theme is the struggle for freedom against tyranny and oppression. In Mary Shelley's *Frankenstein*, it's the hubris of a scientist trying to usurp God's powers of creation. In *Romeo and Juliet*, the main theme is love's triumph over hate. Each of these works also has several readily identifiable sub-themes.

In order to avoid preachiness, it's best to approach the creation of fiction with the idea of simply telling a story. If the story contains Truth—by which I mean universal human truths, verisimilitude, reflection on the human condition—it's very likely that theme will be present and emerge organically from character and situation, without premeditation on the part of the author.

When I began to conceive my novel, *Sutherland's Rules*, I was approaching my sixtieth year and thinking a good deal about aging and mortality. I'd wanted to write a kind of anti-hero, fast-paced thriller for a while, and this idea collided in my head with my concerns about aging to create the driving idea for *Sutherland's Rules*. I loved the idea of having older protagonists in a thriller and giving them free rein to behave like people in the prime of life; of writing a fast-moving novel which would heft a good deal more than simple adventure. The ideas blended together to create the following setup:

Billy Sutherland, an aging, retired dope smuggler, decides to cash in a forty-year-old IOU given him by an Afghani hashish farmer in 1971 after a deal gone sour. At sixty-six, Billy can't do it alone, and so asks his oldest friend, Christian, to help him in this crazy, illegal, and highly dangerous adventure. Billy doesn't *need* the dope, and doesn't plan to sell it: it's all about closure to him, and not going gentle into that long good night.

When I'd let the first draft cool and went back to the book, I realized it was overflowing with theme and sub-themes: aging, unfinished business, the last hurrah before night falls, loyalty, the power of friendship, intergenerational debts of honor, freedom, the surveillance state, geopolitics, faith...not quite what you'd expect from a thriller about two old ex-hippies trying to smuggle a huge load of dope halfway around the world and into the U.K. without coming to the attention of Fortress Europe's police authorities and the U.K.'s sophisticated detection tech.

Now, I'd not set out with the aim of addressing such lofty concerns—my desire was simply to write a cracking good story and have some fun doing it. But looking at the reviews, readers *get* these thematic notes: one reviewer described the book as "life-affirming;" others remarked on the underlying, touching melancholy of these two lifelong friends on what will likely be their final great adventure.

Theme emerges, I believe, because the sincere author can't help putting a great deal of themself into a book; in my case and this novel, that included my reflections on age, mortality, and society. These things are *my* truths. As a result, I believe I ended up with what I'll call "an intelligent thriller", as opposed to the generic thriller where cookie-cutter characters just act out the plot, sowing mindless mayhem as they go.

So when Billy tells Christian, "And look, man, the game—*our* game, our *life*—is coming to a close. Maybe ten more good years, fifteen at most, then it's good as over. I've got my exits mapped out, but I'm buggered if I'm going to die feeling I missed out", he's talking about what any reader who's hit their senior years—and certainly any reader old enough to remember the 1960s—is very, *very* aware of: the final curtain coming down, the finish line clearly in sight, the end of adventure.

Theme matters because *life* is themed. As we blunder through this passion play, we can't help coming to some conclusions, seeing universal patterns and currents, understanding that some things *matter*. When a writer puts all they have of themself—their Truth—into a story or novel, the reader will notice, nod agreement, and care.

Symbolism

Much as I dislike the entire notion of symbolism in writing, there will be those who think the topic needs to be addressed in any serious book on the craft. My feeling is that symbolism is best dismissed altogether by the honest writer. The attempt to find deep meaning in art is the business of academics and critics, and good luck to them. But in most cases, a cigar really is just a cigar.

Like theme, symbolism, where an object or thing is represented by a different one in the story, may simply occur as the subconscious product of a writer's mental process. And as with theme, I believe the author shouldn't invest themselves in the process by trying to consciously seed or place symbolism into a story.

In revision, it sometimes happens that we realize our subconscious has placed some handy symbol in the story—thunder, say, or a wedding band, perhaps a wornout shoe—who knows? The subconscious can kick up all kinds of odd things. If that happens, good and fair; you might even find that echoing this accidental symbology elsewhere, often close to the end, reinforces your story.

One of the best comments on the topic was made by Ray Bradbury.[17] Asked if he sub-consciously (sic; questioner likely mean *consciously*) placed symbolism in his writing, Bradbury replied,

> "No, I would never consciously place symbolism in my writing. That would be a self-conscious exercise and self-consciousness is defeating to any creative act. Better to let the subconscious do the work for you, and get out of the way. The best symbolism is unsuspected and natural."

To the question of whether readers ever inferred there was symbolism in Bradbury's writing which he hadn't intended, and how he felt about it, he replied,

> "One critic thought my vampire family story *Homecoming* was intended as a parable on mankind in the atomic age, under the threat of the atom bomb. I was mostly amused. After all, each story is a Rorschach test, isn't it? and if people find beasties and bedbugs in my ink-splotches, I cannot prevent it, can I? They will insist on seeing them, anyway, and that is their privilege. Still, I wish people,

17   Bradbury's reply to an informal 1963 survey of 150 writers on the conscious use of symbolism in their work. See: http://www.theparisreview.org/blog/2011/12/05/document-the-symbolism-survey/

quasi-intellectuals, did not try so hard to find the man under the old maid's bed. More often than not, as we know, he simply isn't there."

And then there's allegory, a tale in which people are used as symbols for ideas. I value allegory about as much as I value crooked politicians. There's a distinctly false and mechanical taint to the notion of consciously tooling a story in this way that irritates me a good deal.

Reality, Ideal and Actual

How much reality is enough?

First let's clarify the distinction between *reality* and *realism* in fiction. When someone speaks of realism in fiction or of realist literature, they're typically referring to modern fiction, that is, fiction written in accessible language which concerns itself with ordinary people living in the everyday world. Prior to the nineteenth century, literature often centered on the doings of the aristocracy and privileged classes, and before that on gods and supernatural beings. Realist literature, with its focus on the mundane and even banal, developed as a counterpoint to romanticism, which stressed aesthetics and sought to divert the reader from reality rather than reflecting it back at them.

But my concern here is with the depiction of reality in fiction, and specifically *how much* reality is required from us as writers.

Even the most realist fiction is anything but. Take dialogue, for instance. If you were to record and faithfully transcribe the average dialogue exchange between two people, it would be almost unreadable, full of *uh*s and *like*s and *you know*s, hesitations and tics and clichés; so what the writer learns to put on the page is dialogue that *sounds* real but in fact has been carefully processed and structured to convey the impression of realism: it is idealized reality.

So it is with plot. All of us, except for the most fanatical determinists, will agree that real life at least *appears* to be unscripted and unplotted. Stuff happens. And if it seems to us that stuff happens for a reason, it's because our brains are so hardwired for pattern recognition that we'll see patterns even where none exist—which is of course why it's both futile and impossible to argue with conspiracy theorists or religious fanatics. Still, a truly plotless story (and they exist aplenty) is likely to bore or irritate most readers and at best be regarded as an experimental scrap of post-modernism.

Instead the writer, especially the genre writer, presents us with a carefully selected series of scenes and events in which each detail of dialogue and gesture, description and plot, is carefully chosen to fit in with the writer's aim while maintaining the *illusion* of reality. The writer, as God, has created a world in which things mostly happen for a reason, in which people learn and change, in which conflicts are resolved and rewards won. Our writer achieves this by skillful characterization and interactions, and by leaving out anything which would mar the illusion. (It's worth noting in this regard that different cultures have different norms: European readers, for example, are rather more tolerant of moral ambiguity, existentialist concerns, passive protagonists, and loose ends than their U.S. counterparts, who seem to prefer a more rigidly-directed fiction seething with conflict and with everything wrapped up in a nice, tidy bow at the end.)

Importantly, the more fantastic and outrageous the world of their story, the more the author needs to buttress it with closely-observed and precise specific detail about settings, characters, etc. For a fantasy world or an outrageous character to be believable, there needs to be enough sharp detail to make the illusion three-dimensional and solid; it goes without saying that the detail work in itself needs to be interesting for the reader. Writers of the fantastic learn to do this reflexively, but the skill is also a useful one for those whose fiction is set in the here-and-now everyday reality.

One wonderful example of using specific detail to make the fantastic credible is Italo Calvino's *The Distance of the Moon*, the tale of how Old Qfwfq and his friends, back in the days when the moon was much closer to Earth, almost touching it, would row out to sea and clamber up onto the surface to gather moon-milk. Here's a sample:

> *This is how we did the job: in the boat we had a ladder: one of us held it, another climbed to the top, and a third, at the oars, rowed until we were right under the Moon; that's why there had to be so many of us (I only mentioned the main ones). The man at the top of the ladder, as the boat approached the Moon, would become scared and start shouting: "Stop! Stop! I'm going to bang my head!" That was the impression you had, seeing her on top of you, immense, and all rough with sharp spikes and jagged, saw-tooth edges. It may be different now, but then the Moon, or rather the bottom, the underbelly of the Moon, the part that passed closest to the Earth and almost scraped it, was covered with a crust of sharp scales. It had come to resemble the belly of a fish, and the smell too, as I recall, if not downright fishy, was faintly similar, like smoked salmon.*

This level of specific detail is maintained for pages as the story unfolds. Combined with Old Qfwfq's equally detailed digressions and the easy intimacy of his voice, the result is a hypnotic, delicious story that's impossible not to believe.

The other strategy if you really want to tell a whopper is to put the lie (your fantastic premise) right out front in the very first paragraph—even the first *sentence*—of your tale, like this:

I was nine years old when I learned how to levitate.

The beauty of this method is it presents the reader with an immediate take-it-or-leave-it option. They either buy the premise—at least on a trial basis—or they put the book down. And since the reader usually opens a book in the hope of enjoying the ride, the odds are strongly in the author's favor.

As Mark Twain famously put it, "the only difference between reality and fiction is that fiction needs to be credible." The real world has no such concerns, but even the most permissive literary genres (say, science fiction), have their limits. William Gibson said in a 2003 interview that if a few decades ago he'd pitched a novel which included a worldwide pandemic (AIDS), global warming, Middle Eastern terrorists destroying the twin towers with hijacked airplanes, and a white woman competing with a black man for the U.S. presidency, the publisher would probably have called in security to restrain him—and this was before we even got to a worldwide surveillance society and the serial overthrow of leaders across the Arab world.

Fiction, it seems, can only deal with so much reality.

Special Cases: Fight and Sex Scenes

Many authors get into trouble over these, and we've all seen it happen on the page: fight scenes as exciting as numbered instructions for assembling a set of kitchen cabinets, sex scenes so cringe-inducing they make you embarrassed for the author.

When you think about it, there's a lot of similarity in what's going on in fighting and sex. Neither is a rational, willed process like the rest of our everyday lives: when we get into a fight or deep into the throes of passion, older, instinctive, animal processes take over and the higher, analytical functions are relegated to the back seat. A punch comes out of nowhere, you lash out, kick blindly; next thing you're on your back and someone's hands are around your throat. The same with sex: you kiss, and before you know it your partner's hands are tearing off your shirt, a wall slams into your back, you fumble at a belt buckle…

Both activities leave little time for conscious thought, and that should be reflected in the writing. These scenes need to be handled in an impressionistic, realist way, with that molten heat of deep viewpoint penetration; fragments can be put to good use here.

To illustrate my point, here's a passage from a fight scene in my novel, *Sutherland's Rules*:

> *He jerked up, risked his head in the window. There, a silhouette moving into the open. He didn't think, just punched the barrel through the thin glass in a panic and fired a burst, startled by the noise and strobe of red-white as the gun jittered in his hands, and a dark form fell to the ground.*
>
> *More flashes outside, and something zinged overhead, spraying fragments and dust over him as he ducked below the sill. Thwack-thwack-thwack of bullets hitting the far wall, right where Billy was. Christian popped up again, no choice, sprayed the area where he'd seen the last burst, dropped out of sight when the gun clicked on empty. Across the room, Billy was firing short, measured bursts.*
>
> *Shaking hands somehow got the empty magazine out. Oh, shit! He'd left the others on his dresser, and this wasn't the time to cross the room and fetch them.*

The only exceptions to the need for an impressionistic approach in sex and fight scenes are when the PoV character is for some very good reason detached enough to observe the scene. Some highly trained soldiers or fighters actually do experience time flowing slower in the midst of action than we ordinary mortals; a gigolo or a professional courtesan may be able to experience lovemaking more objectively than the rest of us while their client or lover ravishes them. And individuals repeatedly subjected to abuse sometimes learn the ability to check out and be somewhere else entirely as a protective mechanism.

When writing a sex scene, the first thing the author needs to do, as mentioned earlier, is let go of any embarrassment about being judged over what they write. Look, your parents had or have sex too, and so do your boss and coworkers, and I'll bet you a Michelin star dinner that not all of it is vanilla. The only concern you should have is to write damn *good* sex scenes.

I would also encourage you, unless you're going to avoid any onstage sex in your story, to not go all coy and put in a scene break just as things start to sizzle. The reader is paying you to be entertained, and I believe they deserve their money's worth. Multiple award-winning author Michael Swanwick has been known to refer to sex scenes as "reader cookies," and I think that, along with an obligation to ourselves to represent the truth of life, is part of why we shouldn't back off them.

Another consideration is choosing the correct level of diction for the scene. Some characters and genres (hardboiled PI, for example) may employ coarser language than you'd want to see in a YA novel, so it's important to calibrate for both your characters and your audience. But—going back to the talk we had about honesty and self-censorship—nobody in a bedroom is ever going to say, "I want your penis," at least not in my books.

That said, it *is* possible to write a sex scene that is both hot and still tasteful. Authors who aren't writing explicit erotica tend to either keep the sex offstage or else fumble it. To better illustarate my point, and at the risk of appearing immodest by quoting again from my own work, here's a clip from my 2015 novel, *Black Easter*:

> And now she was on him, her hands on his back, in his hair, pulling him to her. His mouth found hers; reason evaporated as reactions long suppressed ignited in the swaying heat of the embrace. Her breasts strained against him in the crush, her thigh was hard against his; the suddenness of his erection surprised him.
>
> Hiss of indrawn breath as she sought him, palmed him. Her flesh was smooth and firm as his hands slid up under her sweater, encountered lace. He eased the fabric off the plump nipple and teased. She pulled off the sweater and pushed his head down, moaning as his mouth closed over her breast. Zippers and clasps yielded, clothes were shed with mounting urgency.
>
> Ignition became firestorm, the bedroom entirely forgotten as she sank to her knees and took him in her mouth. The world tilted and swayed.

As previously stated, you owe it to your readers to represent life honestly, without coyness or falsehood. And your readers will love you for it.

On Style

Style is the way you put your words together on the page. From diction and syntax through to rhythm, dialogue, and other techniques and devices, most of us will develop a distinctive and recognizable style. To illustrate the range of possibility, we're going to look at a few well-known authors; to level the playing field, I've chosen to select openings rather than cherry-picked passages

An author won't necessarily use the same style in every book they write. While we generally do, sometimes a story will require a different approach of us. Whether the decision to adopt a different style is a conscious one or simple instinct, it happens. First person writing, for example, will often demand a certain style to fit in with the voice of the single viewpoint character in the story.

Some authors use plain, unadorned language, short sentences composed of plain, everyday words and nothing more than a comma or period for punctuation. The classic example of this is of course Hemingway, whose direct, declarative style singlehandedly changed English letters forever (and not for the better, in my opinion). Here's the opening of his novel, *A Farewell to Arms*:

> In the late summer of that year we lived in a house in a village that looked across the river and the plain to the mountains. In the bed of the river there were pebbles and boulders, dry and white in the sun, and the water was clear and swiftly moving and blue in the channels. Troops went by the house and down the road and the dust they raised powdered the leaves of the trees. The trunks of the trees too were dusty and the leaves fell early that year and we saw the troops marching along the road and the dust rising and leaves, stirred by the breeze, falling and the soldiers marching and afterward the road bare and white except for the leaves.
>
> The plain was rich with crops; there were many orchards of fruit trees and beyond the plain the mountains were brown and bare. There was fighting in the mountains and at night we could see the flashes from the artillery. In the dark it was like summer lightning, but the nights were cool and there was not the feeling of a storm coming.

For contrast, let's look at the opening passage of John Le Carré's bestselling novel, *Smiley's People*:

> Two seemingly unconnected events heralded the summons of Mr. George Smiley from his dubious retirement. The first had for its background Paris, and for a season the boiling month of August, when Parisians by tradition abandon their city to the scalding sunshine and the bus-loads of packaged tourists.

On one of these August days—the fourth, and at twelve o'clock exactly, for a church clock was chiming and a factory bell had just preceded it—in a quartier *once celebrated for its large proportion of the poorer Russian émigés, a stocky woman of about fifty, carrying a shopping bag, emerged from the darkness of an old warehouse and set off, full of her usual energy and purpose, along the pavement to the bus-stop.*

Here's another master stylist, the incomparable Roger Zelazny. This is the opening passage from his award-winning 1976 novella, *Home is the Hangman*:

Big fat flakes down the night, silent night, windless night. And I never count them as storms unless there is wind. Not a sigh or whimper, though. Just a cold, steady whiteness, drifting down outside the window, and a silence confirmed by gunfire, driven deeper now that it had ceased. In the main room of the lodge the only sounds were the occasional hiss and sputter of the logs turning to ashes on the grate.

I sat in a chair turned sidewise from the table to face the door. A tool kit rested on the floor to my left. The helmet stood on the table, a lopsided basket of metal, quartz, porcelain and glass. If I heard the click of a microswitch followed by a humming sound from within it, then a faint light would come on beneath the meshing near to its forward edge and begin to blink rapidly. If these things occurred, there was a very strong possibility that I was going to die.

And finally, the opening lines of James Joyce's doorstop novel *Ulysses*, hailed as one of the greatest masterpieces of modernist literature:

Stately, plump Buck Mulligan came from the stairhead, bearing a bowl of lather on which a mirror and a razor lay crossed. A yellow dressinggown, ungirdled, was sustained gently behind him by the mild morning air. He held the bowl aloft and intoned:

—INTROIBO AD ALTARE DEI.

Halted, he peered down the dark winding stairs and called out coarsely:

—Come up, Kinch! Come up, you fearful jesuit!

Solemnly he came forward and mounted the round gunrest. He faced about and blessed gravely thrice the tower, the surrounding land and the awaking mountains. Then, catching sight of Stephen Dedalus, he bent towards him and made rapid crosses in the air, gurgling in his throat and shaking his head. Stephen Dedalus, displeased and sleepy, leaned his arms on the top of the staircase and looked coldly at the shaking gurgling face that blessed him, equine in its length, and at the light untonsured hair, grained and hued like pale oak.

Buck Mulligan peeped an instant under the mirror and then covered the bowl smartly.

—Back to barracks! he said sternly.

Joyce's promiscuous use of adverbs and even adverbial tags will not have escaped your notice. And yet if *you* tried this, your critique group would crucify you, and no agent or first reader would likely read even this brief a segment. Even I would raise an eyebrow, though writing this ballsy would certainly keep me reading, and adverbial tags be damned.

You see, none of it matters: all that matters is whether you catch the reader. And since today we have the choice of going indie, writers who don't want to conform and be bound by other people's stifling and myopic rules can and should take chances, develop their style, and tell their stories the way they want to. Just tell a great story in the best way you know how to, use language fearlessly, and own it *all*.

A Brief Note on Grammar and Usage

Like most intelligent, creative children, I hated grammar at school. But as an early and voracious reader, I developed an instinctive understanding of it by osmosis and could tell correct usage from incorrect without being able to explain it; much later, when I began writing, I taught myself the basics.

There are a few items which an editor comes across so very often that their hand twitches towards the vodka bottle when they encounter the same fault in yet another manuscript. Let's look at the worst of these.

1. Authors who Startle

This one really drives me nuts. In manuscript after manuscript, as well as a good few published books, I come across sentences like this:

She startled when someone called her name from the darkness behind the bushes.

No, she didn't.

The problem here is twofold.

First, the writer is confusing the verb *startle* (to surprise) with the verb *start* (to make a sudden, involuntary movement). Second, the verb *to startle* requires an object: you cannot *startle*, you can only *be* startled or startle someone else. Thus:

She started with a yelp when someone called her name from the darkness behind the bushes.

This might be because

She was startled when someone called her name from the darkness behind the bushes.

Or

Someone called her name from the darkness behind the bushes, startling her.

2. "Had" — the Past Perfect Rule

A lot of authors have a problem using the past perfect, *aka* pluperfect, tense (*he had eaten* vs. *he ate*) correctly. This leads to problems such as this:

He had gone to ask her father's permission. The butler had let him in and had told him to wait. Her father had been dubious at first, then had finally come around.

Looking back on it now made him chuckle.

Apart from being tedious to read, this is grammatically wrong. Think of it this way: you need only use the past perfect (he had arrived) *once* at the onset of a scene or event to take the reader from the current narrative time into the narrative past; after that, just carry on in simple past (no "had"). When we're back in the current narrative time, it'll be obvious. So:

He had gone to ask her father's permission. The butler let him in and told him to wait. Her father was dubious at first, then finally came around.

Looking back on it now made him chuckle.

Rule: If you shift into past perfect once, it's good for the whole passage. After returning to the present, if you shift back into the past perfect again (as in a memory or flashback), just do the same: use the past perfect "had" only once, then simple past for the rest of the passage.

3. Lay and Lie

These two irregular verbs constitute a rat's nest for many people, not only writers.

First of all, the verb *lie* has two meanings: to lie down or recline and to tell an untruth. *Lay* also has two meanings: to place something or (colloquially) to have sex.

More confusion arises when you start to conjugate these verbs. Since a good deal of grammar is involved and this isn't a grammar primer, I'm just going to suggest you look these up online or in a reference text if you're in any doubt at all over how to conjugate them in every tense, and make sure you use them correctly in future. This is important if you don't want editors and readers to roll their eyes.

4. The Superfluous "Of"

> *Harold was so depressed at his inability to grasp the simplest rules of grammar that he jumped off of the bridge to his death.*

No he didn't: he simply jumped OFF the bridge. He was *on* the bridge and he jumped *off* it. The of is never, ever required in these sorts of constructions. I don't care if you're coming off night shift, off a high, or off your soapbox, please don't come off *of* it. It's always wrong, no matter how common in spoken American English.

5. The Comma Splice: a Non-issue

A comma splice occurs when two independent clauses (parts of a sentence which could be sentences on their own) are joined by a comma without the support of a conjunction. An example of this would be,

> *Dario wrote feverishly, nothing was going to slow him down today.*

Any copy editor will tell you this is incorrect without the conjunction ("and") to support the comma, and change it to,

Dario wrote feverishly, and nothing was going to slow him down today.

But you know what? I don't care. Nor, I submit, does the reader. The problem with most copy editors (usually because they aren't writers) is that they don't understand that sometimes style trumps rules. There are instances in which comma splices read badly, but it's my belief that they can also punch up flow and imbue a line with an intangible extra something. In my own freelance editing work I make a point to respect a client's style, and not assume every breach of a rule is a mistake: sometimes authors have reasons for breaking the rules. And I've more than once been thanked by an author for respecting their stylistic choices.

6. <u>Commonly Confused Words</u>

Writers endlessly get these wrong, using a word that sounds very similar or identical but has a different meaning to the one they need. If you're not absolutely clear on each of these, pull out your dictionary and write down the definitions longhand so that they internalize.

Affect / effect

Anymore / any more

Breath / breathe

Capital / capitol

Council / counsel

Discreet / discrete

Led / lead

Lose / loose

Principal / principle

Rain / reign / rein

Rack / wrack

Sight / site

Stationary / stationery

Who / whom

Wreck / wreak

This is a very short list. Many more examples can be found with an online search.

Finally, *alright* is just about acceptable in dialogue, but is really incorrect in narrative or formal writing. Use *all right* every time.

Q

FOUR: PUTTING IT TOGETHER

I don't care who likes it or buys it. Because if you use that criterion, Mozart would never have written don Giovanni, Charlie Parker would never have played anything but swing music. There comes a point at which you have to stand up and say, this is what I have to do.

—*Branford Marsalis*

You've finished the first draft of your novel or story. What's needed now is feedback and revision. But first, I strongly recommend you let your manuscript cool off for at least a month or more—and by cool, I mean don't look at it *at all*, and try not to even think about it—to get some distance and perspective. This is essential. In the meantime, researching, taking notes, or even starting to write a new piece of fiction is a terrific idea as it'll help you with the distancing process.

At what point you show your work to others for critique is dependent on how you write. Most of us will want to do at least one cleanup pass before letting others see it; your mileage may vary. So let's look at the whole question of beta readers, critique groups, expectations on both sides, and at what point your work might be ready to hand off for feedback.

Critique Groups

Structuring a Good Writers Group

Writers work in isolation. We're very close to our work. And a piece of fiction is a dynamic, interdependent, sometimes fantastically complex web of forces and relationships. It's therefore vital, as the work approaches completion, for the writer to get outside feedback.

That feedback is called critique, and even professional authors need it. And the people who can give us the best critique are usually other writers (and of course freelance editors, but there will be cost involved).

Forget about the opinions of friends and family; "like" isn't useful feedback for a writer. What you need to know about your story or novel is what's working and what isn't. *Why* and *how to fix it* are icing on the cake.

When in 2006 my wife and I moved to the tiny Greek island of Skópelos[18], I left my San Francisco Bay Area critique group 6,000 miles behind. How was I going to get that vital feedback now?

There are two kinds of critique groups: the face-to-face kind that typically meets weekly, monthly, etc., and the distributed kind where business is conducted online. The former works very well if you live within range of a half-dozen or so other writers. One big advantage of the face-to-face group is the social aspect; writing is a lonely business and a peculiar one, and hanging out with like-minded people is both enjoyable and nurturing—assuming that you have a good, cohesive group, which is by no means always the case. Living as I now was, on an island of 5,000 Greeks and no writers, especially of science fiction, I would have to go online.

There are many established online critique groups. Though some who join them report good experiences, everyone agrees it's very hit-and-miss. Some of these groups are huge and the spread of talent and personalities likewise; there's often also a good deal of cumbersome structure and protocols, not to mention egos and the associated theatrics. I quickly saw that if I wanted a group that was more reliable and responsive, I would have to set it up myself.

If you live in a rural or semi-rural area, or don't like your local writing group(s), my experience may be valuable here.

Like any social group, a writers group is a product of the personalities which compose it, perhaps amplified. Many groups, just like families, are to some degree dysfunctional. The biggest problem areas are typically flakiness, ego, and temperament issues. Beyond avoiding those pitfalls, I also believe the ideal group size is between six and eight members: any less than six (six means a writer gets five critiques) and you risk too narrow a spread of opinion; more than eight, the group becomes unwieldy. I also felt it was important to have a group of writers of at least the same level of craft and skill as myself, which I defined as intermediate or semi-pro.

But an online group across time zones is very different to a face-to-face one in that weekly or monthly meetings aren't necessary, practical, or even sensible. So the tricky thing—beyond finding the right six or seven writers—was going to be setting up a system that was balanced and fair so that everyone received timely critiques when they needed one. Some writers are more prolific than others, and may write at different lengths; some may produce a

---

18   The adventure is chronicled in my nonfiction book, *Aegean Dream.*

short story a month, others two a year; some write two novels a year. How was I going to structure this?

Trust, I thought. Put that right up front and center. Since flakiness and unreliability are the bane of most writers' groups, I decided to make mutual trust and support, loyalty to the group, the core tenet and build outwards from that. Like the Marine Corps' *Semper Fi*, my group would be composed of people who never let one another down.

I began by crafting a constitution for the group, spelling out the expectations and rules, and making sure that everyone understood exactly what they were signing up for We would have no schedule but instead assemble on demand, at brief notice, and our loyalty to one another would be like a blood oath. To underscore that, I named the group *Written in Blood,* and it was very successful indeed, with zero member turnover during a period of five years. Some members are now widely published and have won major awards.

A couple more items if you decide to found your own group. First, be *extremely* selective in whom you allow in: read at least a short story or some chapters of theirs and critique it, and have them critique something of yours. See how they receive and give critique. Be absolutely honest and direct about what the group's needs and expectations are. If something doesn't feel right, pass on that person.

Also, while democracies are good, I believe that one person needs to lead, keep members accountable, and have veto power: the idea of a freewheeling collective is nice, and can work with a small group of perhaps three or four intelligent and collaborative people; but trying to get, say, a dozen writers on the same page is harder than herding cats. Ignore these warnings at your peril.

Next, I recommend you set up a private group on a forum hosting site such as *Zetaboards*, *Proboards*, or some similar free service. This gives you a place to upload files for sharing as well providing a group listserve. (I used Yahoo! Groups but the platform is almost dead now.)

We also found it helpful to have a "crit wrap," i.e., a group discussion period of a day or two once the current crittee had received all their critiques, so they could ask further questions or discuss specific points, as well as generally thank everyone.

However you decide to go about it, if you're serious about writing, I strongly encourage you to find or create a good critique group; you would also do well to look up the many articles and blog posts available on giving and receiving critique. Good critique can make the difference between failure and success, between having your work in print or languishing in a drawer or USB drive. What your mum or your spouse says about your work may give you the warm fuzzies, but it's unlikely to help you; what a good writer tells you is beyond worth.

The Limitations of Critique

It's been said that a writer fluctuates between believing they're the best writer in the world and the worst writer in the world—and in some cases, that they hold both views at the same time.

The point is well-made. When the creative faculty is fully engaged and the characters on the page pulse and kick with life, the writer is in heaven; but when the inbuilt editor that any good writer possesses awakens, or the work runs aground on any of a myriad possible shoals, the writer is convinced the work is crap.

Over the last fifteen years I've founded, participated in, or mentored several critique groups including *Written in Blood*. Though I firmly believe in the standard writers group critique process, I've begun to see its limitations. Bear with me as I approach my point obliquely.

I make no bones about my dislike of the way the publishing industry, steered as it is by suits and the pressing imperatives of the market, is increasingly adopting the Hollywood approach, where everyone gets input on the final result. I personally know of several authors whose book was turned down by a publisher because the marketing department had issues with it (in one case just because it didn't pigeonhole neatly into a category) *despite the fact that the editorial team were unanimous in approving and wanting to acquire it.* And a publisher's decision comes after the work has already been through heaven knows how many rewrites.

My point is that when we try to second-guess, we can always, *always* find issues; and in addressing those issues, we end up making so many changes that we risk sucking all the life and uniqueness out of a work. Today, a book is critiqued and revised, often multiple times, before going to the author's agent, who then initiates a whole new round of revisions; and then the same occurs at the publishing house. This, along with the whole problem of writing dogma endlessly recycled and reinforced through the echo chamber of the Internet and far too many books on writing, not to mention the near-religious belief of many agents and editors that they know how to sculpt a bestseller, is a major reason so many genre novels today seem generic, formulaic, and about as exciting as the kind of art that hangs in bank lobbies and Comfort Inn rooms.

I think that the word "critique" itself is problematic (the etymology goes back to the Greek word, *krites,* a judge) and tends to slant the process towards fault-finding; "evaluation" or "assessment" is probably closer to what a writer needs, but I may be splitting hairs.

Let me be clear: I do believe writers should seek critique, and am not for one instant devaluing the process. But as we grow as writers, we need to be really sure that the type and direction of critique we're receiving is keeping pace with our skills, and that our beta readers "get" our work and our intent. Writers need to be very aware that it's easy to critique anything to death[19]. Tangents and irrelevancies creep in as the well-meaning critiquer casts around to address anything which may raise a question. In this fishing process, things may be caught which materially and subtly contribute to the flavor and uniqueness of the story; and in their doubt, the writer, once alerted, removes or alters the item, and in the process diminishes the final work, bringing it closer to the ordinary.

As an example of this, imagine a Gothic, claustrophobic tale set in a remote castle. In the process of critique, one or more readers is liable to say they want to know more about the world outside. What's going on there? Why doesn't anyone in the castle go down to the village for supplies? Where do they get their water? And so on. These questions may be fair and even relevant, but there's every danger that an insecure writer, in attempting to address them to please some entirely theoretical contingent of readers, begins to put in sentences or scenes or infodumps which degrade the atmosphere of isolation and claustrophobia and consequently lessen the power of the work. Write honestly, and write about what matters to *you*: not everyone may agree, but those who do will respect you for it.

As John Gardner says in *The Art of Fiction*, "Any fool can revise until nothing stands out as risky, everything feels safe—and dead. One way or another, all great writing achieves some kind of gusto."

Even more of a minefield is the advice frequently given in critique about adverbs, flashbacks, show don't tell, etc. While all the standard writing advice is founded on solid principles, it takes true maturity to understand its limits; likewise to know how and when to break the rules.

The point of critique isn't to make the story or book attain some theoretical ideal of perfection based on writerly dogma, but to end up with a publishable piece of fiction which *readers* will enjoy and which communicates the

---

19   The converse also holds true: it's perfectly okay to not find anything to critique. What is *not* okay is to try to rewrite the author's story the way you'd like it to be; critique what's there, but don't try to make it *your* story.

creator's vision in as unalloyed a form as possible. The mature writer needs to have the self-confidence and feel sufficiently secure to say, "no: enough."

Perhaps this is why most pro authors move on from formal critique/open discussion groups and instead pass their manuscripts to a small, handpicked circle of other mature authors for private beta reading, people who they know will "get" exactly what they're striving for and know what the reader wants, rather than taking a scattergun approach to finding fault in the manuscript. The line may be a fine one, but it is nonetheless very real.

To my mind, the best beta readers and editors will understand the distinction between on the one hand fully respecting the author's intent, direction, vision, and style, and on the other, obsessing over some cookie-cutter notion of what the market wants and what constitutes good writing. The focus needs to be on two things only: *what the writer intends*, and *what matters to readers*. Nothing else.

And that's all it ever was about.

Draft Readiness for Betas and Critique

What should a first (or beta) reader draft look like?

The only correct answer to this question is the old English saying, "How long is a piece of string?" The question is a relative one; the answer different in every case.

And yet the question is important to any writer seeking feedback on their work. Because each writer's process is different—sometimes wildly so—from the next's, a first reader draft can be anything from a fairly clean piece of work to a near stream-of-consciousness ramble. I've seen first drafts entirely lacking punctuation; places and names changing semi-randomly; characters unaccountably disappearing or their personalities flipping and seesawing; and subplots appearing and vanishing like quarks in the primordial soup.

The question is one of assumptions and expectations.

Imagine the prospective buyer of a new home arriving to find the walls have only been framed and the sheetrock isn't up yet: they're going to get a bad shock and take issue with the seller. Similarly, unless the reader's expectations are somewhat aligned with the individual writer's concept of a first draft, any critique is likely to be off the mark and there's a good chance one or both parties will be left unhappy and frustrated.

Fortunately, extreme examples aside, there's a bell-curve graph with most writers' beta draft output sitting somewhere in the middle range (in fact, we should probably never show *anyone* an absolutely raw first draft, which I define as a *rough draft*, but rather a 'breathed-over' version, one we've at least done a fast pass through to pick up the most horrid inconsistencies and omissions).

In general, I believe the first reader draft ought to be easily readable and somewhat internally consistent, though perhaps lacking polished prose and/or elaborate sensory and setting description. The major characters should all be present and, on the whole, believable, though goals and motivations may be shaky and need bracing and solidifying; plot and subplots will be visible, but probably unfocused and thin in places; pacing may be patchy, and some scenes will be working better than others; there will likely be structural issues, scenes in the wrong place or missing, too much or too little backstory, and so on.

Unless a beta reader's expectations are correctly set, they're likely to spin their wheels on things that don't matter yet or become frustrated at the uneven and incomplete quality of the work—probably both. I've run afoul of this myself by letting a rather inexperienced reader see an early draft of mine, and they proceeded to comment as though it were a finished work. Expert writers and critiquers will generally make allowances, but it's better to save less experienced readers for final, polished drafts.

Typically what a writer requires of a first draft reader is a "macro," an assessment of the work at a thematic, structural, and character level. Key feedback might include:

- Does the opening hook you?
- Do you buy the premise?
- Is the plot plausible?
- What are the holes in it?
- Are the characters believable?
- Do you care what happens to them?
- Do their goals and motivations make sense?
- Where do they behave inconsistently?
- Does anyone's name and/or appearance change?
- Are the stakes sufficient to keep the reader interested?
- Is the pacing generally okay?

- Where are the flat bits?
- Is the ending satisfying?

Going back to our house analogy, we're definitely not ready to choose paint colors yet. What we're looking for here is to make sure the house is correctly framed with the walls in the right places and the angles true, that the roof isn't going to leak, and that all the main services (power, water, and gas) are correctly located where they'll be needed. So although a brief note that more description and setting detail will be required may be in order, no reader of a beta draft should even consider line-level edits or (heaven help us) typos. All that stuff will get fixed on the rewrites, or the writer isn't worthy of the name.

So the wise writer will prime their beta readers with notes and discuss the kind and level of feedback they're looking for in advance. Even the catch-all, "flag anything that's not working" is okay, though I prefer to be more specific. If you're concerned about a question prejudicing your reader (e.g., "does the protag's plan go too well and the resolution appear too easy?"), save it for the debrief when they've finished reading.

Of course, we also want to know what *is* working, and to hear that we've written a great story or novel; experienced critiquers will leaven and balance their comments appropriately. But ego strokes should be secondary, which is why you should resist showing your work to friends and family (unless they're writers) until it's finished and ready for print. Right now, what you need to know is what's standing between that early draft and greatness.

Drafts and Revision

It's striking just how different in its specifics each revision pass is. Although writers vary enormously in their technique and approach, I think we can make some general observations.

Here's what happens—at least, for me—between the first, rough draft and the final revision pass.

Although I write slowly (1,000 to 1,500 words a day, and my first draft is cleaner than probably the vast majority of authors'[20]), it's still a draft, and substantial revision is always required. The authors who nail it on their first

---

20   I'm not recommending you do the same: in fact I would much prefer to work faster and with more momentum. But it's how I work, and we should all work the way that suits us best.

pass (Kurt Vonnegut reputedly was one, science fiction great Joe Haldeman comes very close) are rare indeed: my advice is don't even think of trying.

The first revision, once you've left enough time for the work to cool, is for most of us actually a partial rewrite, involving sometimes substantial work on characters, plot, setting, pacing, and more. Expect to move, transpose, add, or toss out whole scenes; new subplots may be introduced; information and backstory management will probably need work. In the worst cases, or if the draft was written at breakneck speed (which is why I don't do NaNoWriMo[21]), this revision may amount to a complete teardown.

During the rewrite, wordcount may go up or down. In my own work, I usually find I need to *add* wordage, mostly in the form of description and "stage directions", which I tend to skimp on in my first draft; I may need to amp up stakes and jeopardy, as well as introduce some foreshadowing. Some scenes which feel too "told" or distant will be worked over, made visceral. I fix inconsistencies such as abruptly morphing character names and physical details. And then there'll be factual errors.

The second revision pass is usually easier and more limited in scope. During this stage, I typically find myself fine-tuning character motivation and behavior; adding still more interiority and deep PoV judgment; and tweaking dialogue so that it's more distinct and true to character, trying to make it snap and crackle.

This is a good time to strengthen my theme, by which I mean asking myself what the book or story is really about, and making sure that I reinforce this wherever possible within the context of believable character and action. I also find myself noticing words and gestures I tend to overuse (the dreaded, 'he/she nodded/smiled/sighed,' etc.).

On my final revision, I'm getting very granular and looking at the fine detail: I'm copy and line editing, looking to smooth every bump and buff out the most minor defects. This polishing pass isn't about what the story *is* and how it unfolds, but rather about how I present it to the reader in a way that's efficient, engaging, and pleasurable. Many authors, especially those looking to be traditionally (i.e., non-indie) published, will find themselves needing to trim their manuscript further, as publishers can be quite inflexible on wordounts.

By this last pass, I should have a very clear vision of who my characters are and what my story is about. I'm still tinkering with dialogue, ensuring that's

---

21   *National Novel Writing Month*, which occurs from the beginning to end of November each year.

it's as crisp as can be and watching for redundant, leftover words from earlier revisions, as well as malapropisms and the like.

But most of all, I'm looking to make the prose really sing, within reason- Where I once used to think a sublimely lyrical prose style was everything, I now care at least equally about telling a great *story*, because I think that's actually what readers want. It's what *I* want when I read. (More on perfectionism later.)

What do I mean by making the prose sing? Well, since by this stage I've (hopefully) eliminated scene-level structural issues with regard to pacing and plot, I'm now looking at rhythms and relationships in the prose itself at both paragraph and sentence level. As I read, I'm looking to see if my these are properly structured and sequenced in relation to their neighbors as well as internally.

Next, is the syntax working? Do I repeat words? Can I improve on word choice, strengthen verbs, punch up a metaphor, fine-tune any serendipitous symbolism I find I've included, perhaps work in some echoes and resonances, tightening the invisible wires that bind the story together? Have I committed unconscious rhymes, or clunky sequences of sentences that all begin with the subject ('*He* did this. *It* was Monday. *He* did that. *She* said this. *The cat* grinned.')? Are there words or even sentences I can cut? Are there still filtering words that can be lost and replaced with the stronger, more visceral perception of free indirect speech either literal or metaphorical (e.g., replace, 'he felt very tired' with, 'he could sleep for a month')?

Finally, as I work my way through the story, I'm looking for small slips and inconsistencies in both voice and tone.

Voice needs to work at every level: dialogue, interiority, and narrative. It needs to be true and consistent to each character. Skill at handling voice is critical to making readers care about a character, as well as keeping them engaged during breaks in the action.

Tone, that slippery thing we defined earlier on as the overall effect, quality, or mood of a work of fiction, the sum result of theme, voice, prose, and much else, needs to be precisely calibrated throughout: a dark theme approached in a sober voice may yield a tragedy; but a humorous, upbeat voice will change the tone and transform it into black comedy. The point here is to understand what tone you're trying to achieve and not break the effect with false notes or drastic, unintended shifts. You *must* be in control of both voice and tone.

And now? Omigod, it's...*done!* After this final revision, all that should remain is close proofreading (best left to others), and the work is ready to go out and earn its keep in the world.

How I Learned to Stop Worrying and Love the Rewrite

Oh, the horror! The horror!

I'm not sure about Joseph Conrad—history does not tell—but I'm prepared to bet that a majority of writers whimper at the prospect of revising their work, especially if the revision involves structural rewriting. The thought of having to do something akin to removing, remodeling, and replacing several floors of a high-rise without the whole building collapsing is daunting, to say the least. And what about all the plumbing, electrics and ductwork that run through the floors you're refitting? How will changes on those floors affect the rest of the building? It's enough to make you crazy.

As any writer knows, it's not over when you write, THE END. It's a glorious moment, to be sure, and one to be savored—but it only means you've completed the first draft and, after giving the work time to cool, will soon be getting to grips with the dreaded rewrite.

Writers, as I mentioned above, come in all kinds. There are those of the down-and-dirty first draft persuasion whose prose floods onto the page so fast they can barely keep up. I admire these people for the sheer energy and momentum of their attack—they can often get four to five thousand or even more words on the page in a day. I don't envy them the task of rewriting, which is quite possibly going to be even more work than the first draft! That said, it's easier to strip down and rework rough writing than prose that's almost good enough to publish already.

One reason rewrites are scary is the "I'm done with this!" factor—which, after spending several months or even years in labor with your novel, is not unreasonable. And the work of revising your manuscript seems so much less glorious and magical than birthing the thing in the first place. It feels as though there's a good deal more analytical than creative process needed in the rewrite, so the notion doesn't seem so exciting. That's not strictly true, but let's take it a step at a time.

You take a good, hard look at the raw love-child you've delivered your muse of, and maybe had some writer friends offer their two cents on, and you discover that there's room for improvement. Your antagonist is half made of cardboard, and why on Earth would the empowered female protagonist risk her neck for a guy who's an insufferable misogynist? You could drive a truck through some of the plot holes—*nobody* can swim three miles in 45-degree water towing a mini-submarine by a rope between their teeth, and the cultural mores of Mongolian yak herders are *not* going to be those of twenty-somethings from the San Fernando Valley. What *were* you thinking?

You grit your teeth and fix the obvious things, the easy stuff. More research may be needed, and quite probably more stage directions and character work. But even after you've done all that, something still isn't working, or you have no idea how to address something that's been niggling at you.

Be patient, because at the darkest hour, magic happens. A character suddenly reveals the motive for which they said something, took some action, or made a key decision. You see a connection between two story events that casts an entirely new light on a pivotal plot point. You understand why you wrote a particular scene that appeared to have no immediate meaning at the time. You realize that you have two characters transposed, that one should be doing this particular action, not the other. Your characters that just an hour ago looked like stick figures begin to take on form and solidity.

Before long, the entire work which just yesterday felt like a pile of dry, lifeless bones comes alive under your hands. Tendons and muscles appear from nowhere, the loose collection of bones tightens and snaps into an ordered skeleton. Flesh begins to cover it, it acquires a face; and pretty soon your formerly dead creation is breathing and moving and talking. Despair turns to elation, defeat to victory.

What's happened of course is that your muse has once again delivered the goods. By just keeping at it, showing up at the keyboard and doing the patient, steady work of a craftsman, your subconscious mind (and that *is* the muse, the place where the magic happens) has had the time and been given sufficient raw material that it's now delivering a whole new level of output to you in the form of insights, explanations, connections.

I believe that most writers—except perhaps those who indulge in very detailed outlining and plotting in advance, to the point where their process is more mechanical than organic—rely largely on the subconscious to do the heavy lifting. When I write my first draft, I have an idea of where my plot may go, and often extensive notes on my characters, but I can't yet see very far or deep. Characters will do things I don't quite understand at the time, and the plot will take odd turns I couldn't have foreseen. This doesn't mean I have no control: I do hold the reins, but loosely; and on the whole, I find I hardly ever need to tighten them and rein in the team—they seem to know where they're going better than I do. Somehow I get to the end.

My point here is that what's happening is that the writer's subconscious uploads data to their conscious mind in successive waves. During the first draft the conscious mind is putting down on paper a somewhat garbled version of the narrative that the subconscious, the muse, actually has worked out in great detail (this correlates nicely with the "found object" school of plotting). During the rewrite, the muse or subconscious looks over what the blinkered conscious mind has put down on the page, laughing in some places and frowning in others. It then decides to take a long nap.

Stephen King compares writing a novel to rowing across the Atlantic in a bathtub: you're alone with no land in sight. I'd add that it's dark, and there are storms and monsters of the deep. Fear and self-doubt pluck and worry at you constantly. As is so often the case with writers, especially novelists, despair is never far away. You know you suck, and pretty soon the whole world will know it, too. Maybe you should just bury the manuscript and take up knitting.

After a little more time in which you might find yourself spinning your wheels and seriously considering those knitting classes, your muse wakes up and starts delivering the goods. Suddenly you're energized. You slap yourself upside the head and wonder how you could have been such an ass as to not see this, and get that so wrong. You make the connections, your fingers fly on the keyboard. The magic is happening.

Revision will not be always easy or fun, but it's vital work that will make the difference between a great book and a dull or so-so one. And those rewrites you once feared become something you look forward to.

On Process

Making Time to Write

I've been known to frown and harrumph when people say they want to do something but just don't have the time. Look, *nobody* has time, except for teens and maybe those who are unemployed. But we make time for those things we really want to do by triage and prioritizing, by stealing that time from something that's less important than the other. For many people, the first thing to do is claw back time spent online or in front of the TV.

I write in the early morning, riding a strong caffeine buzz and, more importantly, before my head gets filled with rubbish words from the world around me (and our air is thick with rubbish words; they come at us from everywhere, from the roil and rattle of the news and the lies of politicians to the poison of advertisers and people's whiny, self-absorbed social media postings. But I digress).

I'm freshest and least likely to be interrupted in the early morning. If you're a night person, that works too. There's a psychic quiet at night, when the household is asleep and the world outside is settling, that's very conducive, so long as you still have some gas left in the tank. Whatever. *Just make the time*. If other people are taking it all, learn to say *no* more often. If you don't make the time, you'll never be a writer.

But I don't have children, or have to beat the rush on a long commute: I work from home. If I had a commute, a train one, I might choose to write then. A train, like a coffee shop, can be a productive place to work, its rhythms and bustle providing just that kind of white noise that some people need to focus inward.

I recognize that for all of us, sometimes life just presses too hard, from everywhere, at once. Young children, elderly parents, health or emotional issues, moving home, a new job…all these things can defeat the best intentions, no matter how sincere. Nobody should make themselves ill: at these times give yourself a pass, don't beat yourself up, and take care of the real priorities. It's like dieting: you need to know when to be kind to yourself. Just don't let it derail you for good, and get back to work as soon as you've dug your way out. It's a blip, not the end.

Enabling and training by habit the ability to focus inward is one of the most important things a writer can do, and there's no right way other than the way that *works for you*. In fact, a good deal of any writer's work—and this is often hard for those around us to deal with—involves staring into space and letting the mind roam, sometimes for long periods.

Some writers take this to extremes. Douglas Adams's process was apparently to build the entire book in his head. He would procrastinate as long as humanly possible ("I love deadlines. I love that *whooshing* sound they make as they fly by"), spending hour after hour in the bathtub, until finally, when circumstances forced him to it, he'd sit down and bang out a draft in a matter of days. Alfred Bester's process was somewhat similar, composing in his head till there was nothing left to do but "grab my hat and run for the typewriter."

Now, I can't hold a whole book in my head, and likely you can't either. So we must work in more pedestrian ways, thinking and taking notes, a process of steady, daily accretion as we build our first draft.

ℚ

One Author's Process

This is how I work. Take what's useful and ditch the rest. I'm not saying *do this*, just *do something*: find what works for you and stick with it. So:

Out of the mists of mind, a situation arises, a character comes knocking, and I'm intrigued. I test the idea to make sure that it's more than just that, that there's a story there. Really: it took me a long time and a good many stalled early stories to realize that an *idea* and a *story* are two very different things. A tornado that rips a house off its foundation and dumps it and its young female occupant down in another land is an idea (or a situation); Dorothy's struggle to return home, and the challenges she must overcome in order to do so, are the story. You can test the idea by asking yourself whose story this is, what their goal is (and why), and what's standing in their way.

If there's a story, and chemistry between characters and author, I begin taking notes in longhand (longhand feels so much more forgiving and playful), mostly on my characters. Then I look for the ending and maybe a few way-points, just to have a very rough framework for this new house: four posts and a roof are all I need. (I know, I know. But sometimes you just have to throw your hands up and allow a mixed metaphor...I mean, we're friends by now, right?)

After a few days or weeks of note taking, I can start writing. I go for 1,000-1,500 words a day, and can usually hit that in two or three hours. This is a fairly leisurely pace, but the upside is that my first draft comes out pretty clean. I'd like to write faster to maximize energy and drive, but like most things in writing, there are no hard and fast rules. Those great writers I mentioned who revise little or not at all? The amazing part of that—to me—is that they get the structure right the first time round. We ordinary mortals should be so lucky.

Still, even a thousand words a day will result in a standard-length novel (80,000-90,000 words) in three months or so. The important thing is regularity. I strongly believe that habit and discipline are the two things that give a writer, especially a newer one, the best shot at successfully producing good work. It doesn't matter if you write in the morning or at night, during your lunch break or on the train, in the garage or a coffee shop; it doesn't matter if you write your draft in a mad, unpunctuated stream of consciousness or in measured, grammatically and syntactically perfect paragraphs. What's important is to write daily and to have a target you hit or exceed as often as you can. By doing this you'll not only train yourself but also begin to train those around you (family, roommates, whomever) by establishing a regular writing time and place. It may be hard, and sometimes everything will conspire against you. But if you want to be a writer, you'll make the hard choices and not only carve out the time but also ensure, by whatever means necessary, that your writing time and space is respected and remains free of interruptions.

When the story's cooled and I've reread it and fully digested the notes from my trusted beta readers, I first of all try to pinpoint exactly what the story is about—in other words, theme. The answer should be very clear, and admit of brief, unambiguous definitions, like *crime doesn't pay, freedom comes at a price*, or *there's no place like home.* Knowing this when I begin my revision will allow me to prune and cut out stray tendrils and offshoots and make the entire work point in the same direction.

Next, I go through the manuscript and do a scene-by-scene, "after the fact" outline of what I have. Armed with this three- or four-page structural overview, it's much easier to follow the plot thread and spot breaks, missing connections, loose ends, and all the rest. I note where I need to move, add, or delete scenes, introduce or alter plot events, etc.

If we agree that the writing process is entirely dependent on a collaboration between the conscious and unconscious mind, then the whole success of the process is founded on communication. What's your creative subconscious trying to say in this story? And when you took dictation and wrote that first draft, how much did you get right? You're working—or should probably be—fast in a first draft. You're going to make mistakes. Get over it.

Whenever I've looked back over my own novel or story drafts after allowing them to cool, it seems to me that, at some level, the *whole story is there*, but in the process of transcribing that raw unconscious material, I've put things in the wrong place or left something out: I've *misheard.*

I repeat: at some level, the whole story is there.

In the process of revising one novel, I realized that I had two characters *exactly reversed* in their major traits—no wonder they weren't working! As soon as I switched them around, everything they did suddenly made sense. But it was all there to begin with.

Similarly with plot: although some of the plot events may not be working in my early draft, when I look carefully at my setup and all the strands available to pull on, I often find that all the elements are in place for the fix—like a jigsaw, the pieces were there all along, I'd just been trying to fit the wrong pieces in the place. Once I realize that, the fix is easy.

Many rewriting issues, from plot to dialogue, can be solved by examining your characters and making sure they're fully alive, real people complete with their own hopes and fears and agendas. If a character isn't working or isn't behaving credibly, look critically at their goals and motivations, which is where the deficiency is often found. Revisit their bio and backstory—in short, breathe life into them.

Of course, there are side-effects and repercussions to any changes you make, and you're going to have to track those diligently and make adjustments as required throughout the story. And some of the solutions will take time; my advice is, don't force the pieces. But do talk to your characters, and listen to them. All the time.

As for the more minor mechanics of revision, I suggest you keep a copy of every major draft and dump your deletions and cuts (at least those you're fond of) into an 'out-takes' file. But don't be afraid to make cuts, even whole chapters, including those scenes or lines of dialogue or description which—although they no longer work—you think you can't bear to get rid of. "Kill your darlings!" goes the old advice, and I think it's okay advice up to a point[22]; you have an inexhaustible supply of imagination, and will find lines every bit as good or better to replace them with.

Priming the Pump

Before I start a writing session I always spend a short while—perhaps fifteen or twenty minutes—either reading some fine prose or, more often, poetry. So indulge me while I talk a little about the value of poetry to the writer. Fortunately for you I'm no academic, and lack the erudition to bore you with tedious analysis.

Right now, I'd bet half my audience is preparing to skip the rest of this chapter, but dig: I was turned off poetry both by school and by encountering awful examples of the stuff, too. But I believe anyone who wants to write ought to at least give poetry a chance *as an adult*—and I mean *good* poetry,

---

22 There's a puritan school of writing that says that if an author really loves a scene or descriptive passage or piece of dialogue, it needs to go (presumably on the grounds that it's overworked or something). I say, *nuts*. By all means look at it: you may find you really are guilty of mannered writing (writing that draws attention to itself) or some such sin. But in general, I think this is the mindset of those that advocate giving up everything that's fun in life on the grounds that privation and suffering somehow makes you a better person. I'll keep my vices *and* those passages I love, thank you, and to hell with dogma.

not fluff. How do you know if it's good? It's good if it quickens your pulse or sends a shiver down your spine; if it's stood the test of time, far outliving its author, it's likely very good indeed.

We should read great poetry because it's drenched in magic and speaks of immortality; because it frees us from the ordinary, giving us a glimpse over our claustrophobic modern horizon, or possibly even beyond the veil. And because it just delights.

If you're a writer, you should read poetry, maybe even try your hand at it, because nowhere will you find metaphor, compression, and precision of language to equal the best poetry. I'll quote seven brief fragments here, hoping you'll savor the words with me, and rest my case there. Read slowly, let them get under your skin. Or feel free to skip ahead.

The force that through the green fuse drives the flower

Drives my green age; that blasts the roots of trees

Is my destroyer

—Dylan Thomas, *The Force that through the Green Fuse Drives the Flower*

❧

But pleasures are like poppies spread:

You seize the flower, its bloom is shed;

Or like the snow falls in the river,

A moment white—then melts for ever;

Or like the borealis race,

That flit ere you can point their place;

Or like the rainbow's lovely form

Evanishing amid the storm.

—Robert Burns, *Tam o'Shanter*

❧

Never on this side of the grave again,

On this side of the river

—Christina Rossetti, *A Life's Parallels*

❧

There is one story and one story only
That will prove worth your telling,
Whether as learned bard or gifted child;
To it all lines or lesser gauds belong
That startle with their shining
Such common stories as they stray into.

—Robert Graves, *To Juan at the Winter Solstice*

☙

I saw the best minds of my generation destroyed by
madness, starving hysterical naked,
dragging themselves through the negro streets at dawn
looking for an angry fix,
angelheaded hipsters burning for the ancient heavenly
connection to the starry dynamo in the machinery of night

—Allen Ginsberg, *Howl*

☙

— Then do the clouds like silver flags
Stream out above the tattered crags,
And black and silver all the coast
Marshals its hunched and rocky host,
And headlands striding sombrely
Buttress the land against the sea,
— The darkened land, the brightening wave —
And moonlight slants through Merlin's cave.

—Vita Sackville-West, *Moonlight*

☙

This is a wild land, country of my choice,
With harsh craggy mountain, moor ample and bare.
Seldom in these acres is heard any voice
But the voice of cold water that runs here and there
Through rocks and lank heather growing without any care.

No mice in the heath run nor no birds cry
For fear of the dark speck that floats in the sky.

—Robert Graves, *Rocky Acres*

When the Going Gets Tough

Just Let Go

Learning is a funny thing.

Beginner's luck is a very real phenomenon. The very first time we attempt a thing, and this surely includes writing, we often do very well: by not having preconceptions and a head full of rules, we act spontaneously and without artifice, and in the process come up with a result which—however lacking in technical sophistication—is true, and may even be Art.

After that, things usually go downhill. Encouraged by the first, surprising result, we want to understand more, to learn rules and skills. We buy a book on the subject. Maybe we take a class. Suddenly, it's as though we've taken a bite of the forbidden apple: where before was only innocence and sponta-neity is now duality, the awareness of success and failure and the means to judge it…which we, if not others, surely will. Where before we were playing, we now have to struggle within a framework of rules and judgment. Play becomes work, and that's the kiss of death for creativity, the point at which so many lose heart.

You can see this process at work in any adult activity class. Initial high en-thusiasm, then a sudden, big drop-off. Most of the remainder will stumble on for a little while, dropping out by ones and twos in the weeks and months that follow, until at the last a core of just 20 or 30 percent of the original en-rollees is left. If the teacher is a poor one, or the mix of students unfortunate, the class will just die off.

As writers, if we're serious, we quickly start submitting work for publica-tion, starting with the top markets in our chosen genre. We begin collecting rejections, impersonal form letters at that. And though the toughest, the tenacious few, will grit their teeth and carry on, most of us eventually lose heart and turn to something less punishing.

One thing I've found useful is to *act as if*, to *pretend* that we have the chops we actually don't yet; as science fiction author Pat Cadigan once told me, "Show me what you wish you had."

Now, there's a lot of motivational hooey out there that suggests that this technique generates some kind of cosmic vortex of opportunity, which is fine if you want to buy into that—I don't. But what it *does* do is free you up, give you the space to play again, allow you to act spontaneously. It changes your line of attack from timid to confident, from negative expectations to no expectations, from fear to fun. Let go of rules and fears and hit that keyboard in the spirit of Nabokov or Cordwainer Smith, William Gibson or James Joyce, Tom Wolfe or Roger Zelazny. Go for it. Take risks. Have *fun*.

After years of just fooling around on guitars, I took lessons for a while. One-on-one, with a teacher I greatly admired. As a somewhat compulsive perfectionist with high expectations of myself, I was nervous to the point of paralysis at every lesson; try as I could, I couldn't relax, which totally stopped me feeling the rhythm or getting into any kind of groove. I was a terrible student, and eventually dropped out.

At home, away from my poor teacher's laser gaze, I one day just let go, attacking the instrument with spirit and abandon, sacrificing technique for sheer heat; I wanted to *feel* what it was like; so I pretended, convincing myself, just for a moment, that I had all the chops. The effect was a revelation. Before long, I found rhythm and beat, I started to sound good. I'd rediscovered the spirit.

Like gas in an engine, there has to be something to power our efforts, and I believe that thing is our spirit, our creative impulse. *You gotta have fire.*

This is a technique you can apply to writing. I'd likely be wrong if I told you you'll turn out deathless prose on your first try, but I promise that if you write faithfully, from your heart, hitting the page with the spirit of a samurai, the results will be both surprising and motivating. Yeah, you're probably going to have to step back once in a while, but if you can begin to incorporate spirit into your work, you're more likely to both enjoy it and not hamstring yourself from the get-go. Fear and timidity are Art's deadliest foes.

The Bad Place

Sometimes writing is so difficult that all you can do is laugh. The laugh is not one of humor, but more like that of Holmes as he goes over the Reichenbach falls, or perhaps one of Lovecraft's characters as he fully realizes the depth of the unspeakable cosmic horror which is about to devour his soul.

Every seasoned writer is, I think, deeply mistrustful of anyone who claims to love the process—I mean the entire process, especially the in-the-trenches bayonet-work, when you're locked in a life-and-death struggle with yourself and every fiber of your being screams *give up, surrender, you can't win*, because each sentence you craft, each line of dialogue, is worthless, stilted nonsense. At these times there's nothing to love about the process, and to hell with inspirational quotes and touchy-feely nonsense. All you have is will and determination, and it had better be up to the task.

There are times when any of us who are honest with ourselves wonder why we're doing this.

Perhaps you worked like a dog on that last novel, and it's lying dead in the water. You feel nobody gives a damn for your work. The competition out there is so brutal you can't even get an agent to read your query, let alone your novel. You'll never break through, no matter how hard you try. You wonder why you're doing this when you could be doing something fun. You're a fool. You're beat. You want to reclaim your life.

Writing is a tough gig. Darwin red in tooth and claw. If you're like me, you go to this bad place periodically. You have your pity party, kick and scream and pound and cry…and pretty soon you square your shoulders and get back to work.

It's okay to have doubts and fears.

When I go to the bad place, I look hard at my reasons for writing. If I told you I didn't care about earning money at it, I'd be lying. Of course I care. But that's not why I write. Bear with me while I fill in some backstory.

I was lucky with my very first book, *Aegean Dream*. The book sold exceptionally well in the U.K. and was picked up by a foreign publisher as well, selling over 11,000 copies to date. All through one glorious summer, fat checks were rolling in monthly. It felt great. Before that I'd only sold a few science fiction short stories for beer money; now I was somebody!

My second book, *Sutherland's Rules*, released in early 2013, was a brutal reality check. Although everyone who reads it loves it and asks for a sequel, and the reviews are great, sales have been very disappointing, in the low hundreds. I went into a funk. I'd put my heart and the best part of a year of my life into this book—what the heck happened?

Well, for one thing I'd switched not just genre but a whole category, going from a nonfiction travel memoir to a thriller. Worse, *Sutherland's Rules* is a very quirky thriller, really an action-adventure/suspense/buddy-caper/police procedural with a shimmer of the fantastic around the edges, and featuring older protagonists to boot! Effectively, I was starting all over again, with an oddball book in a far more crowded category.

But I wasn't giving up.

I began working on another novel, a supernatural thriller. By then I'd started publishing other people's novels through my micropress, Panverse Publishing, and that, coupled with the need to work part-time, ate up every second of my time and more. The novel I'd written 30k words of got abandoned. I was a failure, a pretend writer.

Somehow, crazy as life was, I managed to get a few new short stories written, tidied up a few others, and glued them together into a collection, *Free Verse and Other Stories*. The collection got some good reviews, and even plaudits such as "a writer who deserves wider recognition" and "underappreciated writer." Sales to date? Not much over a hundred copies.

Go to the bad place. Do not pass GO, do not collect $200.

What went wrong?

Collections are never an easy sell, even for name writers. Also, this was a science fiction collection. Never mind that a few people thought it a strong volume, I'd switched genres again! Oh, sweet Jesus, would I never learn?

I went back to the abandoned novel, *Black Easter*, and just a few months later wrote those glorious words we all love, THE END. I was a writer again, and now I'd written a second novel in the same genre (thriller)!

But why? Why do this? The chances of success in this game are not good, and I'm not young. So why be a writer when I could be hiking, playing my guitars, visiting art galleries, taking photographs, learning East Coast Swing…

I write because I need to. Because there are stories I want to tell, characters and situations I want to read about which nobody else has written. Because I want to share these stories with other people, perhaps intriguing and even delighting them in the process. Because the high of getting fan mail from a total stranger whose life I've touched is worth any number of lows. Because I want to leave a legacy of some sort. Because I have this weird idea that if a creative person stops doing what they feel driven to do, something inside them will sicken, and that hurts the soul.

And I write as an indie because I want be in charge of my creations.

It's okay to go the bad place. Like a warrior, a writer needs courage, and plenty of it. But courage isn't the absence of fear, it's facing our fears and carrying on in spite of them. Go to the bad place, explore it, despair in it. And when you're done, come back.

And besides, there's always a chance that the next book will be a bestseller.

Have the Last Laugh

I have a deep dislike of self-help and motivational books, videos, speakers, gurus, and the like. Don't get me wrong—I'm every bit as prone to fits of existential angst as the next person. But I'm fundamentally a stoic at heart. I believe we're all essentially alone, and we had better damn well be self-reliant and self-fixing, however unfair the world and however personal a hurt may feel. I worry that anyone who follows motivational speakers, or fervently believes that watching self-help DVDs is going to help them, is probably going to remain broken: worse, they're giving up their freedom of thought. It's the first step on the road to brainwashing by cults.

There are, however, two books I occasionally refer to, the first for a chuckle and to get perspective, the second because it makes me feel sane, since just about every quotation in it reinforces my own philosophy and approach.

The first, *Pushcart's Complete Rotten Reviews and Rejections* is an indispensable little volume not only for writers but for anyone who enjoys seeing self-important people (in this instance, critics and publishers) proved deeply, desperately wrong in their reviews and rejections of great authors and of books which went on to become classics. A few examples:

> *OTHELLO (Shakespeare): "Pure melodrama. There is not a touch of characterization that goes below the skin."*
>
> —*George Bernard Shaw*
>
> *WUTHERING HEIGHTS (Emily Brontë): "Here all the faults of Jane Eyre (by Charlotte Brontë) are magnified a thousandfold, and the only consolation which we have in reflecting upon it is that it will never be generally read."*
>
> —*James Lorimer in the North British Review*
>
> *CRASH (J.G. Ballard): "The author of this book is beyond psychiatric help."*
>
> —*Rejection letter*
>
> *THE SPY WHO CAME IN FROM THE COLD (Le Carré): "You're welcome to Le Carré–he hasn't got any future."*
>
> —*Rejection letter*
>
> *THE TIME MACHINE (H.G. Wells): "It is not interesting enough for the general reader and not thorough enough for the scientific reader."*
>
> —*Rejection letter*

HEART OF DARKNESS and *YOUTH (Conrad):* "*It would be useless to pretend that they can be very widely read.*"

—*The Manchester Guardian*

Remember that the people who penned these rejections are the same ones who today believe that you can apply templates to fiction, and that they can tell winners from losers. These are the same people who send *you* rejections.

The second book is an equally delicious little volume titled *Zen Guitar* by Philip Toshio Sudo; you don't have to play guitar to enjoy it, you just need to have a pulse. The book consists of a number of quotations from famous musicians, followed by a one- or two-page commentary from a Zen perspective by the author; each one is a gem and applies equally to our own craft—just substitute the word *fiction* for *music*. Some of my favorites (you'll have to buy the book for the commentaries) are:

"*I don't think you can ever do your best. Doing your best is a process of trying to do your best.*"

—*Townes Van Zandt*

"*If (you're) going to sweep the floor, sweep it better than anybody in town. And if you're going to play the guitar, really, really, really get in it, and don't be jivin'.*"

—*Carlos Santana*

"*Music should go right through you, leave some of itself inside you, and take some of you with it when it leaves.*"

—*Henry Threadgill*

"*You can build a wall to stop people, but eventually, the music, it'll cross that wall. That's the beautiful thing about music—there's no defense against it. I mean, look at Joshua and fuckin' Jericho— made mincemeat of that joint. A few trumpets, you know?*"

—*Keith Richards*

On Writer's Block

As someone who's had real and recent struggles with a difficult-to-write novel, I want to talk a bit about writer's block.

Let me say right up front that I don't believe there is such a thing *in the sense most people apply the term.* I think the popular image of writer's block—and one that's shared, unfortunately, by a good many writers—is that the muse has abandoned the author. Even taken as a metaphor, I don't feel this is a helpful definition. Why? Because it's disempowering. It makes the writer the victim of a mythical entity with superhuman powers.

It's natural for a writer who suddenly can't make headway to panic. Unfortunately, not only is that likely to result in even greater paralysis and stress, but it's distracting you from the real issue.

First off, a muse, which I believe is actually the writer's subconscious, requires work on the part of the writer to nourish.[23] This work primarily takes the form of sitting down every day at the keyboard, whether or not you feel inspired, and typing something. In addition, the writer needs to be reading, getting out, exchanging ideas, experiencing life, and generally feeding their muse. If you sit around waiting to be inspired, you're likely to have a very long wait, and any inspiration that does come is likely to be short-lived.

I think the well of creativity *can* temporarily run dry, especially after a long spell of intense work. If you really believe writing burnout is your problem, worrying isn't going to help. Better to simply accept that you need to recharge. Go for long walks. Go on a reading binge. Travel. Have a torrid love affair. Try bungee jumping or Go-Kart racing. Or even simply allow yourself time to get bored. Just living and experiencing life will help far more than fretting or obsessing or trying to force something to come.

I'm going to assume you've already assured yourself that your story idea will actually carry a novel, trilogy, etc. If the answer is yes, all well and good; if no, maybe you need to do some radical retooling, or possibly even pass on this particular work.

Writer's block, especially with a work-in-progress, is almost always a signal from the subconscious that something isn't working, and specifically that the writer doesn't understand some specific aspect of what they're trying to write. I always look for this first in character and ask myself if I have all my characters squarely in focus, whether I know them all as well as I should. Since I don't plot much in the abstract but rather let my characters create the plot under pressure from a strong setup, the problem for me is likely to do

23   Stephen King and Damon Knight talk at length about this.

with character…because if the characters aren't moving and acting, the plot stops. If I don't fully understand their goals and motivations and internal conflicts, how can I write the next scene? I want to write about real people, not puppets. Digging deeper and earnestly into character can solve a lot of story issues and unblock you.

It's also possible that the blocked writer is simply bored with their work. This happens. In this case one answer is to write an exciting scene even if it's out of sequence: this can often get you engaged and moving again. Don't feel compelled to write those boring bits, look for workarounds or, as Elmore Leonard recommends, *leave them out*.[24] If they bore you, they're very likely to bore your reader too.

On a related note, it's also worth asking yourself how much you care about the story, whether your heart is really in it. Newer writers in particular may find, on honest reflection, that they're trying to write something they think will be popular rather than telling a story they truly want to tell. You need to have passion about the work for it to come alive.

Sometimes writer's block can be a result of the writer's own growth process. As we start learning our craft, our appreciation and admiration of others' talents, and the realization of how much we don't know and still have to learn, can amplify our self-doubt to the point where it becomes a paralyzing wall of fear. This is something that makes or breaks writers, a demon that comes with the territory. It's helpful and reassuring to remember that every single one of the writers you read and admire also had to learn their craft and overcome these same terrors[25]. They say it takes a million words to learn your craft, and I believe there's some truth in that. It's also good to bear in mind the saying that "it takes ten years to become an overnight success."

Or the writer may simply be overwhelmed by life. Demands of work, money concerns, young children, domestic discord, caring for aging parents, health issues, all consume time and bandwidth: by the end of the day you're too fried to do even think, let alone write.

My advice in these cases is the same advice I gave above: unless you're absolutely tapped out, try to write daily and first thing in the morning, before your head gets filled with junk and other people's words and the world begins to pull you every which way. Get up an hour earlier if you can. Find the courage to say *no* to everything that's not critical. Ditch TV and get your social media and online time under control. All these things can be huge time sinks.

24   The actual quote is, "Try to leave out the part that readers tend to skip."
25   Robert Silverberg, in "Science Fiction 101", gives a wonderful, detailed account of his own struggle to master his craft.

I can hear the chorus now: "But how am I supposed to relax?" Nuts. If you want to write badly enough, you'll push other things aside. Think how much more relaxed you'll be when that stuck novel you're stressing over is done!

Fear of failure can be a factor, too. Writing is a hard, solitary business. You ask yourself if the possible returns—because, honestly, very few of us will ever make anything like a living off our writing—are worth the effort. Hell, you could be having fun: playing games, hiking, watching movies, partying with friends, learning some other skill. Instead, you're stuck at your desk trying to pile up tens of thousands of words about made-up people which, in the end, nobody may give a damn about. Well, those doubts are real, and we all face them at some point, often more than once. My approach is to face them squarely, stare them down. It's *your* decision, nobody else's. You can choose to go forward, or you can stop. So far, I've chosen to go forward.[26]

When you're stuck, look to your characters. Listen to them, let them tell you why they're having trouble moving forward. Sometimes you'll find the character arcs have become tangled and require a little combing out to restore them to separate threads before you can begin to braid them anew.

If your tale is set in the real world, try using Google Street View to walk the streets your characters walk, to see their neighbors' houses and the locations where things happen. This can really help get the creative imagination flowing again and spur progress. You have to be *in* your story, standing right by each character as you write about them, to forge ahead. When you're stuck, it's often because—like Timothy Leary—you're on the outside, looking in.

Sometimes all the above isn't enough. You have to dig deeper still, farther than you ever have, to get to the core of what was the story is about. Stephen King, in *On Writing: A Memoir of the Craft*, has a superb anecdote about a tough encounter with writer's block that stopped him for weeks halfway through writing his masterpiece, *The Stand*. Once he'd identified the problem, the solution he hit upon was simple, elegant, and memorable.

Finally, talk to people you trust. Your spouse, fellow writers, your ideal readers. Simply doing that, talking through your problems and fears, can bring fresh insights on what is actually causing you to be stuck and can help you move through it.

26   I disagree with all the writing coaches and bloggers who exhort and badger you to keep writing at all costs: I believe that knowing one has a choice and the freedom to stop if the cost–mental, emotional, or otherwise–becomes such that your life suffers is empowering, and I'm not going to take that away from you. You need to *choo*se to keep writing, not do it to please me or anyone else.

To conclude, then, writer's block comes in many forms, and each is eminently capable of a cure. But it takes effort, intelligence, courage, and, most of all, determination to work through them. Writing is mostly about tenacity and will. The only one who can finish the work is you. And though your muse may feel like some fickle, external supernatural being, they're not: they're a part of you, the writer.

Writing is hard. But with courage, creativity, and sheer willpower, you can break through any block.

The Trap of Self-Censorship

Among all the fallout from the original Edward Snowden/NSA revelations was a 2013 PEN America survey[27] of 520 writers which found they are "not only overwhelmingly worried about government surveillance, but are engaging in self-censorship as a result." The survey states:

– 24% have deliberately avoided certain topics in phone or email conversations.

– 16% have avoided writing or speaking about a particular topic and another 11% have seriously considered it.

– 16% have refrained from conducting Internet searches or visiting websites dealing with topics that may be considered controversial or suspicious and another 12% have seriously considered it.

Not long after reading that, I came across an indie author's post about why he no longer swore in his books. Although the author goes on to give several lengthy and occasionally credible artistic reasons for the decision, he candidly admits that part of his reasoning includes the concern that some readers are turned off by coarse language, and that he'll probably sell more books if he stops using it.

My reaction to both the above? I don't ^%#+\@*^ believe this! What are we coming to?

Last case first. It's true that the gratuitous overuse of coarse language can be obnoxious, attention-seeking, and a crutch for poor writing, especially in dialogue. And some fine writers, among whom Charles Portis (*True Grit, The Dog of the South, Norwood*, et al), arguably one of the very best American

---

27   Titled *Chilling Effects: NSA Surveillance Drives U.S. Writers to Self-Censor*, the full survey is posted online

authors of the twentieth century, have written several books without using a single swearword.

It's also true that bad language can alienate some readers. One reviewer of my own book, *Aegean Dream*, says in his review, "I might have given this a fourth star had it been written with fewer profanities/vulgarities." (Meh. One reader. There are probably less than a couple of dozen cusswords in the whole 350-page book.)

All that said, the truth is that people in real life, even the best brought-up people, do swear, often, and almost without exception when bad things happen. Some people even go so far as to use swearwords as punctuation. This is reality, people. And I take the firm view that it's the writer's duty, even in fiction, to represent the reality of the world.[28]

The same thing goes for sex. In the real world, most adults spend a substantial amount of time thinking about sex, and—all things being equal—enjoy practicing it whenever the opportunity arises. It therefore follows that if you're writing fiction for grownups, at some time or another your characters are going to think about, or have, sex. And yet I can't count the number of times I've listened to newer writers agonize over writing a sex scene out of concern that a parent/relative/boss/coworker will end up reading their book, and what will they think of them as a consequence.

In fact, if the reader in question is also a grownup they won't probably think anything negative about the author—unless the sex scene is badly written, in which case they'll just think the author is a poor writer. But if the scene is done well and feels like reality, they'll probably appreciate the honesty. Because the truth is that readers, with the possible exception of overly Puritanical and religious types, respond very well indeed to honesty, including hot bedroom scenes and, where appropriate, coarse language. It's part of making the fictional dream real, people!

In the case of the PEN America survey, the concerns are of a different order, with the writers surveyed fearing that they'll be tagged, flagged, and perhaps even targeted by the authorities.

While there's some sound basis to these concerns, the fears aired also show a high degree of ignorance about the way intelligence works. Simply running a few web searches on terrorist training camps, white supremacist groups, or the enrichment of uranium for use in nuclear devices is not going to land you on a watch list or bring a SWAT team to the door.

---

28   Stephen King addresses this same point wonderfully in his book, *On Writing*; John Gardner has a whole chapter on honesty and truth in *The Art of Fiction*.

In the course of writing *Sutherland's Rules*, my 2013 caper novel,[29] I did no end of research—online, in library books, and via phone and email with experts—on drugs, smuggling, Afghanistan, the Taliban, intelligence and police agencies, customs procedures, surveillance techniques, and much more.

If all this activity ran up enough flags (unlikely) to be brought to the attention of a human intelligence analyst, it's just possible they checked it out, built a profile, noticed I was an author, and concluded I was researching a book on the subject; if not, the publication of the book would have confirmed this. But more likely it didn't even come up on the human radar, because the reality of modern-day intelligence is that the amount of SigInt (intelligence gathered by interception of signals) is so fantastically vast that even a small fraction of it would swamp all available human resources. Face it: you're both less unique and less important than you think. And, although mistakes can occur, these people are generally smarter than people give them credit for.

So the likelihood of a few innocent queries getting you into trouble is, really, insignificant; if, however, your contact list includes firebrand Imams, terrorist suspects, or known felons, then, yeah, all bets are off, and you may even deserve a little attention from the authorities.

It is true that there's always going to be some small chance that you'll get flagged, and perhaps suffer some minor harassment down the road as a result of repeated digging into very sensitive areas. But you know what? Art isn't safe. Artists and writers and journalists around the world daily face beatings, arrest, and even death, and it doesn't stop them. Because honesty is more important to them. If you want safe, you're in the wrong business.

To me, a big part of honesty—in fact, the biggest part of being an artist or writer—is having the courage of your convictions. I'd bet a year's income that a great many of the PEN survey respondents who self-censor and fear to run web searches on "topics that may be considered controversial or suspicious" also claim to be supporters and admirers of Burmese opposition leader Aung San Suu Kyi, Russian feminist punk rockers Pussy Riot, Martin Luther King, and Nelson Mandela. Does that smack of hypocrisy to you?

And yeah, this shouldn't happen in the U.S.; but, like earthquakes and tornadoes, it sometimes does. Get over it. If you don't like it, vote; if that doesn't work, protest. But if you protest, don't be wimps like Occupy, who cut and ran at the first snow flurries in NYC and the first threats of muscular action from the authorities. In Russia, crowds of protesters will stand

29   The protags in my novel *Sutherland's Rules* risk both life and freedom in pursuit of love, loyalty, and their ideals.

all day in temperatures of 20 below; in other countries, they regularly face tanks and tear gas and rubber bullets. But writers in the U.S. self-censor because they fear getting an extra pat-down or some intense questioning at the airport next time they fly, or having their activities monitored a little more closely? Give me a break.

So are we going to be honest as writers, or leave it to those of real conviction?

The Best and Worst Writing Rules

….by which I mean these eight "rules" manage to be both at the same time, depending on how you apply them and whether you just choose to believe what others tell you, or instead question them and reach your own conclusions. As an exercise—the only one in this book, as I'm not big believer in reductionism—I'm just going to list these with no commentary appended. I've addressed most (but not all) in my text, and encourage you to reflect on them and then, using the following two blank pages, take a few minutes to write your own notes on why each "rule" is both good and bad at the same time.

- Write what you know
- Show, don't tell
- Open with action
- Don't use flashbacks, especially at the start of a work; if you must use them, keep them brief
- Get all your viewpoint characters onstage in Act One
- Protagonists must always be active, never passive
- The bad guys get all the breaks
- Conflict in every scene

Write what you know

Show, don't tell

Open with action

Don't use flashbacks, especially at the start of a work; if you must use them, keep them brief

Get all your viewpoint characters onstage in Act One

Protagonists must always be active, never passive

The bad guys get all the breaks

Conflict in every scene

Favorite Authors' Writing Rules

And now that we're done demolishing the entire *corpus* of received wisdom from tens of thousands of contemporary writers, bloggers, literary agents, screenwriters, publishing sales executives, and every single blinkered editor and movie producer out there, let's conclude by seeing what a handful of really great writers think is important to a story.

Mark Twain

1. A tale shall accomplish something and arrive somewhere.

2. The episodes of a tale shall be necessary parts of the tale, and shall help develop it.

3. The personages in a tale shall be alive, except in the case of corpses, and that always the reader shall be able to tell the corpses from the others.

4. The personages in a tale, both dead and alive, shall exhibit a sufficient excuse for being there.

5. When the personages of a tale deal in conversation, the talk shall sound like human talk, and be talk such as human beings would be likely to talk in the given circumstances, and have a discoverable meaning, also a discoverable purpose, and a show of relevancy, and remain in the neighborhood of the subject in hand, and be interesting to the reader, and help out the tale, and stop when the people cannot think of anything more to say.

6. When the author describes the character of a personage in his tale, the conduct and conversation of that personage shall justify said description.

7. When a personage talks like an illustrated, gilt-edged, tree-calf, hand-tooled, seven-dollar Friendship's Offering in the beginning of a paragraph, he shall not talk like a Negro minstrel at the end of it.

8. Crass stupidities shall not be played upon the reader by either the author or the people in the tale.

9. The personages of a tale shall confine themselves to possibilities and let miracles alone; or, if they venture a miracle, the author must so plausibly set it forth as to make it look possible and reasonable.

10. The author shall make the reader feel a deep interest in the personages of his tale and their fate; and that he shall make the reader love the good people in the tale and hate the bad ones.

11. The characters in tale shall be so clearly defined that the reader can tell beforehand what each will do in a given emergency.

12. An author should say what he is proposing to say, not merely come near it.

13. Use the right word, not its second cousin.

14. Eschew surplusage.

15. Not omit necessary details.

16. Avoid slovenliness of form.

17. Use good grammar.

18. Employ a simple, straightforward style.

Elmore Leonard

1. Never open a book with weather.

2. Avoid prologues.

3. Never use a verb other than "said" to carry dialogue.

4. Never use an adverb to modify the verb "said"…he admonished gravely.

5. Keep your exclamation points under control. You are allowed no more than two or three per 100,000 words of prose.

6. Never use the words "suddenly" or "all hell broke loose."

7. Use regional dialect, patois, sparingly.

8. Avoid detailed descriptions of characters.

9. Don't go into great detail describing places and things.

10. Try to leave out the part that readers tend to skip.

11. My most important rule is one that sums up the 10.

12. If it sounds like writing, I rewrite it.

Kurt Vonnegut

1. Use the time of a total stranger in such a way that he or she will not feel the time was wasted.

2. Give the reader at least one character he or she can root for.

3. Every character should want something, even if it is only a glass of water.

4. Every sentence must do one of two things—reveal character or advance the action.

5. Start as close to the end as possible.

6. Be a sadist. No matter how sweet and innocent your leading characters, make awful things happen to them—in order that the reader may see what they are made of.

7. Write to please just one person. If you open a window and make love to the world, so to speak, your story will get pneumonia.

8. Give your readers as much information as possible as soon as possible. To heck with suspense. Readers should have such complete understanding of what is going on, where and why, that they could finish the story themselves, should cockroaches eat the last few pages.

Neil Gaiman

1. Write

2. Put one word after another. Find the right word, put it down.

3. Finish what you're writing. Whatever you have to do to finish it, finish it.

4. Put it aside. Read it pretending you've never read it before. Show it to friends whose opinion you respect and who like the kind of thing that this is.

5. Remember: when people tell you something's wrong or doesn't work for them, they are almost always right. When they tell you exactly what they think is wrong and how to fix it, they are almost always wrong.

6. Fix it. Remember that, sooner or later, before it ever reaches perfection, you will have to let it go and move on and start to write the next thing. Perfection is like chasing the horizon. Keep moving.

7. Laugh at your own jokes.

8. The main rule of writing is that if you do it with enough assurance and confidence, you're allowed to do whatever you like. (That may be a rule for life as well as for writing. But it's definitely true for writing.) So write your story as it needs to be written. Write it honestly, and tell it as best you can. I'm not sure that there are any other rules. Not ones that matter.

❧

FIVE: TAKING THE PLUNGE

"A tree cannot find out, as it were, how to blossom, until comes blossom-time. A social growth cannot find out the use of steam engines, until comes steam-engine-time." —Charles Fort

So You Want to be Published?

Why? Why do you want to be published?

No, really. I'm serious. Just humor me as I go out on a limb here.

During a brief Google search a few years ago to see what the Internet community's collective wisdom on this question might be, I was surprised to find that the question doesn't seem to have been aired much. One of the very few posts I found on the subject came from a writer who—as well as saying they "want to be read" (fair enough)—went on to say, "I'm trying to raise money to get an editor to read my work." Uh-oh.

It's no exaggeration to say that the desire for publication assumes *geas*-like proportions. Beginning writers (I was one, and can attest to this) are absolutely desperate to be published—so much so that they'll ignore all the advice and red flags posted everywhere on the Internet and on writing sites and get suckered into parting with thousands of dollars by scam-artist editors and publishers. The hunger to be published seems at times like one of those biological imperatives, on a par maybe with the need for food, shelter, and sex.

In the spirit of questioning assumptions and examining our own motives— which I've always believed are healthy things to do—let's take a step back and try another question: "Why do you write?" Since writing is, for a vast proportion of us, difficult, lonely, and very time-consuming work, this is a reasonable question. And given the very low hit rate among aspiring authors and the slim chance of ever being able to make a living it, we could arguably be doing more rewarding and enjoyable things with our time.

On the positive side, the desire to write and be published is the same as that which fuels any creative pursuit. Writers are motivated by the same hungers that drive musicians, painters, and other artists: an earnest need for self-expression, for creation. But whereas I don't think anyone learning their first chords on a guitar really thinks they're ready to go out on a stage before an audience, the new writer has no such inhibitions. They somehow lack objective measures, or the yardstick necessary for self-assessment (which is why a critique group of the best writers you can find is so terribly important).

On the cynical side of the scale, I'd wager that a good number of those who set out to be writers are motivated by dreams of wealth and fame, of bestseller stardom, complete with quietly adoring librarian groupies and appearances on *Fresh Air*. Somehow, society does nothing to dispel this fantasy, and maybe it shouldn't. Why, after all, should anyone question dreams and puncture aspirations, however misguided, when the world will likely do so far more decisively? And it's quite possible that the aspiring writer driven by illusions (or delusions) of wealth and fame may transmute, in the course of practice, into the honest artist seeking self-expression.

So is the answer, "I write because I want to be read" good enough? I don't think so. To me, it indicates that the person hasn't looked deeply enough into their motivations. I'd even hazard that such a person isn't really suited to the task, since all good writers are, in my experience, people possessed of powerful and searching intellects who ask the deep questions and don't flinch from them. If there's one quality that defines a writer I'd say it's curiosity, and most especially curiosity about people, about what makes them tick, act, and react in a given situation.

Perhaps the most—indeed the only—valid answers to the question, "why do you want to write?" are, and have always been, that there are stories you want to read which nobody else has written. That there are characters and ideas you want to explore. That you have to write, because if you don't, something inside you will hurt, sicken, even die. It's a need, a compulsion, entirely unrelated to public success.

What about publication, then? Why are we so desperate for it, like children who just have to have that puppy so badly they can't think about anything else? Where does that compulsion come from?

Validation is the first thing that comes to mind. Okay, but let's be realistic. I'll confess right away that in my first year or so as a writer I—like almost every other new writer wannabe—sent stories to the *New Yorker* and other equally stratospheric markets. This is very like taking an evening class in CPR and expecting to pass your certification exam and become an M.D. the next day. This doesn't mean that validation or, more properly, a benchmark by which to gauge your progress, isn't necessary, but it should be sought at an appropriate level.

Publication is also about income. All of us driven fools who choose to be writers would love to quit our day jobs and make a living at it. I mean, *dayum!* who wouldn't want to make a living inventing stuff and making made-up people have adventures? It's like being paid to be a kid again (except, of course, for the hard work, self-doubt, and grim loneliness of the task). And yet, I think money should be the last thing on the writer's mind while they're about their business, because trying to write with the express desire to make a killing is only going to kill one thing—your story.

Where does all this leave us? Once we've asked and honestly answered these deep, uncomfortable questions and decided that the reason we write is because some strange force is driving us to do it, and we'll do it even if the work is hard, lonely, and peculiar, and we might never make a penny at it, and it may be our fate to simply labor on in obscurity, with nobody ever taking an interest in our work, and we do it, in the end, like a child lost in play with their toys, humming distractedly to themselves while creating elaborate adventures for people only they can see…then, just then, I believe something great might emerge.

Trad or Indie?

One of the signs of Napoleon's greatness is the fact that he once had a publisher shot.

—Siegfried Unseld

I'm betting that at various points throughout this book at least some of you have been thinking, yeah, I get it, but how am I ever going to get my novel published if I don't play the game like a good little writer and follow all the industry rules and expectations? Well, it's pretty simple: you either go indie ("self-publish," as it used to be termed), or you take a deep breath and start querying agents anyway.

For some reason I can't entirely fathom—except for the fact that we're a bunch of barely-evolved monkeys—it seems that everyone feels a need to take sides on this issue. When I first wrote about making this decision in 2012, there were still those who claimed that agents and publishers were the shining guardians of quality, the last barrier between legions of innocent readers and an ocean of vile dreck; several years on, I suspect nobody, even in the industry, can credibly claim that anymore. Among the indie books which have become world-class bestsellers are E.L. James's *Fifty Shades of Grey*, Andy Weir's *The Martian*, and the *Wool* trilogy by Hugh Howey.

The truth is that the traditional publishing model is broken, deeply flawed, and needs to go away. There are many agents and people in publishing who care deeply about trying to give newer authors a chance; but the likelihood of anyone who isn't already a name getting a book deal is so slim, and the road to publication so time-consuming, burdensome, and peppered with potholes, that I can no longer advise anyone to go the traditional route.

Still, some writers cling to the need for validation they've been taught to associate with a book deal. They may have concerns about the stigma historically attached to indie (a leftover from the days of the vanity presses), or not want anything to do with the business side of book promotion and distribution—and I understand that. They want to get into lots of bookstores and have a publisher go to bat for them, get them reviewed in the mainstream media, and arrange book tours.

Let's look at all this.

One of the huge changes that began in the publishing industry around the millennium and has accelerated steeply since the depth of the recession back around 2010 is that instead of investing small sums in cultivating promising writers over time, publishers are cherry-picking a few authors who they think have that magic *something* and throwing six- and seven-figure advances at them,[30] along with keeping their current Big Name authors happy.

Unfortunately, this all comes at the expense of what is called the midlist, that huge stable of new and existing authors whose books sell moderately well but aren't—at least yet—ready for stardom. The midlist, publishing's middle class, has been put on starvation rations and is on life support. Not only are current midlist authors not getting their contracts renewed, but much less money is available to invest in new authors.

Still, you might get lucky. New authors do sometimes land book deals. And although advances vary enormously, somewhere in the $10,000 range may be considered a very rough average for a first novel.[31]

---

30   Interestingly, if you take a half-decent book by an unknown and give them a seven-figure advance, the media attention *alone* will pretty much work to make that book stand out and climb the charts. Feel free to be as disgusted as I am by this cynical practice.

31   You don't get the loot all at once. It comes in stages, usually on signing, on turning in the completed work, and on publication; and your agent typically gets 15% of the advance.

That sounds, great, right? What's the problem here?

Well, to begin with, you've put several hundred—possibly well over a *thousand*—hours of your life into that novel. That's not counting the time and emotional energy—scores, possibly hundreds more hours—that you've spent on researching agents, crafting individual queries to each, following up, and on and on.

Doesn't matter! Finally, an agent bites. They not only read your chapters, they ask for a full…and astonishingly, they *love* it. Congratulations! You're probably already one in ten thousand.

This, however, is just the beginning. The agent will likely want some rewriting. After that, they'll shop the book around. Back goes your number into the hat, and with a lot of luck an editor will love it. That editor will consult with people in sales and marketing, and if it fits nicely into a category and everyone's on board, they'll get back to you, probably with further rewrite notes and requests.

No problem, you say. You send the manuscript back, and if you're very lucky you'll get decently copyedited too. Your book is on its way to publication.

If everything goes well—that if to say if your editor doesn't leave, or get fired and replaced by one who hates your book, and you get a good cover—your book will, somewhere between a year or two after it was accepted, be in bookstores.

Unfortunately, a lot of things which a new or midlist author once took for granted, like reviews, a decent marketing budget, and perhaps even a book tour, may well not materialize or meet your expectations. It's not uncommon for books to be released with near-zero marketing and promotional support, and even name authors aren't guaranteed widespread reviews today: there are just too many books, perhaps a third of a million traditionally published and up to twice as many indies a year in the U.S. alone. And books don't remain in the bookstore long; between three and six months after publication, your book, unless it does well, will vanish from the stores.

Now, a book released without some muscle behind it is unlikely to sell enough copies to earn out its advance. That not only means you get no more money but, since sales numbers are logged, your chances of selling the next novel are materially reduced. Your own publisher set you up to fail.

And I've simplified the process a lot so as to not bore you. Did I mention the social media platform of thousands a new author is expected to have and curate? Anyway…

If you decide to go the indie route, the chance of success isn't necessarily greater. You do however have a number of advantages, which include:

- Complete control over just about everything, from your story to cover and interior design

- A short road (weeks to months) to publication once your novel is done

- No contracts or obligations to anyone

- Full access to sales data in near-real time

- Regular, predictable payments from Print-on-Demand (PoD) and digital sales channels

- Typically much higher royalty from each sale, especially on ebooks

The downside? Well, you either have to do everything yourself, including cover design (not advisable), or at the least pay for a copyeditor and a graphic artist, for which you should budget a *minimum* of $1,000, and probably $2,000-$3,000 to get the book into really good shape.

The actual publishing process itself, especially through Amazon's Kindle Direct Publishing (and, for other channels than Amazon, Smashwords, D2D [Draft to Digital], and IngramSpark offer additional platforms and distribution resources), is easy and free.[32]

You also have to do all your own promotion and marketing...but again, as a new author, the amount of support you're going to see from a publisher—unless you're anointed as one of this year's handful of Chosen Ones—is likely to be negligible.

But what about brick-and-mortar presence? Don't sweat it. For a reality check, ask your friends, family, and co-workers how many print books they bought in a physical bookstore over the last year as opposed to buying from an online retailer in either hardcopy or digital format. Times have changed.

Ultimately, the only things that matter are:

1. Do you have any objective measures (friends' and your mom's opinions don't count) that lead you to believe your work is really ready for a wide readership?

2. Are you prepared to invest a lot of time and a moderate amount of money in preparing, polishing, and formatting your work to professional standards and learning the ropes?

---

32   IngramSpark charges a small fee for setting up titles for PoD.

3. Are you temperamentally suited to the endless self-promotion and multiple other tasks required to succeed?

If the answer to these three questions is *yes*, then indie is certainly your best choice.

A Tale of Two Manuscripts

To reinforce my argument above, let's look at two case histories (*war stories* might be a better term), one in traditional publishing, one in indie publishing.

Around fifteen years ago, I was hired to do the initial, fairly substantive, copyedit on a self-help book written by a friend, a medical practitioner with a very successful practice specializing in stress management and hard-to-treat hormonal disorders. He had the knowledge, he had the platform (critical in the nonfiction arena), and his timing was perfect.

I helped him put together a proposal, and before long he'd snagged an agent. The agent did some further editing, buffing the book till it gleamed. After doing the rounds, the book was acquired by an imprint of Penguin Putnam.

Initially, it was a love-fest. My friend was offered a $20,000 advance, a healthy sum for a first-time author, and was told he'd get strong marketing and promotional support. The editor assigned to the book said it was the best-presented book she'd ever seen and that it was good to go.

But then, an editor who had summarily rejected my friend's book just months before while working at another publishing house was hired by Penguin Putnam and put in charge of the imprint.

As the book inched towards production, the whole deal turned frosty. The book was given a truly awful, generic cover that made it look like a technical manual; my author friend was allowed no input on the title; the person assigned to do the press release on the book didn't read it, and asked my friend to write his own press release; and the book—despite the hefty advance paid—received no marketing support from the publisher beyond sending out a few reviewer copies. They were going to let it sink or swim on its own.

My friend, a very proactive man, isn't one to flounder for long. When he saw what was happening he talked to his agent, who pointed him to a PR firm that promised the moon. Faced with the need to self-promote, my friend signed a contract with this company, which specializes in setting up radio and magazine interviews for authors. He spent the next several months working his butt off writing articles and doing interviews at all hours with countless obscure small-town radio stations and local papers. At the end of the contract, he'd spent over $40,000 of his own money on marketing.

The book never earned out its advance. My friend's comment on the publishing industry? "I'd be very happy to see them all go out of business. I've never seen an industry that's more incompetent."

Now let's look at the other side.

Indie publishing, dear reader, is hard work. I speak from experience: in the decade since I founded Panverse Publishing, I've published four science fiction and fantasy anthologies, three novels by other authors, two of my own novels, my nonfiction book, *Aegean Dream,* and this volume.

I'd originally taken *Aegean Dream* the traditional route; after all, here was a non-genre, mainstream book, a bittersweet true story that read like fiction set on an idyllic Greek island, the very island that the mega-hit movie, 'Mamma Mia!' was shot on. The book featured food, love, eccentric locals, intrigue, corruption, social commentary, an antagonist, and even cameo appearances by Pierce Brosnan (the movie was shot during our last months on the island). Its theme—escape from the rat race to a Greek island—is a universal one. And finally, it wasn't the typical, sugary, *A Year in Provence*-type travel memoir, but an honest, tragi-comic true story. I believed I had a very marketable book, and had every confidence I'd do better publishing it via the traditional route. I was also fortunate in having a pro critique group who took my first drafts to pieces and pointed out a number of issues, all of which I addressed in the book's many rewrites.

A good many agents bit on my query but balked at the book's length—the manuscript was 135,000 words, at least 35,000 words over length for the category. One agent complained it didn't fit the formula, and was too unvarnished (by which he meant I told too much truth: go figure). But eventually I found an agent who utterly loved the book and felt it was good to go as it stood.

After a dozen or so rejections from major and midsize publishing houses, all of whom said the book was well-written but the travel memoir category was overfull, or the book didn't quite fit the category, or it was too long, I'd had enough. I decided to publish it through Panverse, my own imprint.

I'd done several stints of freelance copyediting over the years and didn't need help in that area, but I hired a professional graphic artist for the cover. By the time *Aegean Dream* was published, in July of 2011, it was clean, well-formatted and nicely packaged in both print and digital form, a professional-quality book in every respect.

For six months, hardly anything happened. I sold a couple of hundred copies and couldn't get the book reviewed anywhere, despite the fact that I had some short story credits and a track record as an editor of well-received anthologies. I'd sent out fifty or sixty hard copy ARCs (Advance Review Copies) with crisp, professional press releases and blurbs to reviewers and book bloggers and *not a single one* replied or reviewed—you can bet the books all went straight into the recycle bin. Yes, even if your book is professionally copyedited, proofread, and has an attractive, well-designed cover, mainstream reviewers still won't touch you: I understand they're buried in books, but the taint attached to indie among these people is both pervasive and strong.

Then, in January of 2012, after the point at which a publisher would have pulled the book from store shelves, I noticed an uptick in sales. It began slowly, going from a book every day to two, to four, five...and by midsummer to a very healthy peak of twenty copies a day, six hundred a month, on Amazon U.K., where it remained the #1 nonfiction book on Greece for over three months, getting well into the top few hundred Kindle books on several occasions.

Aegean Dream did all of this with no marketing and no reviews, beyond those that readers volunteered on Amazon. In under four months, the book sold over two thousand copies. Five years later it's still selling a few hundred copies a year. And not a single reader has complained that it's a long book!

The book did well for several reasons. One, I happened to write a book with the potential to appeal to a wide demographic; two, I believe that after years of writing and critiquing and editing I was ready as a writer; and three, as an editor and self-publisher, I did everything possible to put out a high-quality finished product. As a result, when, near the end of the gloomy British winter, U.K. readers thinking about holidays in the Greek isles started looking for books on Greece and found and subsequently enjoyed mine, they told friends; and growing word-of-mouth, along with rising Amazon visibility, bootstrapped me the rest of the way.

I picked these two anecdotes because I have personal knowledge of the details. From everything I've read and the many writers I've spoken to in both camps, I'd say that my friend's experience with traditional publishing, while perhaps not typical, is far from unusual; he did everything right but was unlucky. My own self-publishing experience, on the other hand, is atypical, an outlier: I did just a few things right, and I got lucky.

A Cautionary Note

There are people out there who've parlayed their way onto the speaking circuit and written books with the usual banner-headline titles about how to become a blockbuster author and all the usual snake oil; you might learn something from them, but in my view they're just peddling more dogma and lining their pockets in the process.

Others have founded dubious "author services" firms which charge stiff and sometimes exorbitant fees for editing, cover design, book packaging, and the like, often subcontracting them out to poor schmoes who are paid low-end industry rates.

The reason to be wary of these people is that they're insiders who know better than anyone how very tough the market is and how limited the slots for new authors in trad pub; but they've understood that there's far money to be made in selling, often brokering, author services than by writing or working in publishing itself. I say this as someone who makes part of his living as a freelancer providing editing, copyediting, and print formatting services; the difference is that I have a conscience, and I give a damn. For too many people, the newer author desperate to publish is a mark to be fleeced, a walking dollar sign with a target a yard wide across on their back.

It's also worth noting that the vanity press, the charge-to-publish scammer, has, even in the era of indie, never gone away. In fact, they've flourished, and in some cases partnered with the scoundrels mentioned above.

For this reason, Victoria Strauss's *Writer Beware* blog (simply Google it) is a must-read. I very strongly recommend that you check it out before paying for *any* "author services."

ⱺ

CONCLUSION

I don't think we have much choice about whether we're writers or not, and perhaps not even about what we choose to write. But we do have absolute freedom to choose *how* we write: we can blindly follow rules and fashions, hammering our material into false shapes out of timidity or to please others, or else we can question and analyze every assumption and so-called rule we encounter and decide for ourselves what to use and what to discard.

The honest practice of any art forces self-knowledge; the process, if pursued, becomes self-sustaining, a feedback loop. If you strive for truth in your writing and write for *you*, from your heart and with humility, you'll succeed. How you measure that success is up to you, nobody else. But I guarantee that if you work hard and apply your intelligence and passion, you'll produce the best work you can, and it will be unique and true.

The choice, dear reader, is yours.

∂ ∂ ∂

Author's Note

Thank you for buying *The Fiction Writing Handbook*. I do hope you found it a helpful guide to the craft.

As an independent author, I don't have the support of a marketing department or big publisher: I'm wholly dependent on readers like you to spread the word. If you enjoyed my book, please consider doing one or more of the following:

- Write a review, however brief, and post it online

- Tell your writer friends about this book, or gift them a copy for their birthday

- Follow me via my blog at dariospeaks.wordpress.com or my Amazon author page at amazon.com/Dario-Ciriello/e/B002UF67GY

Thank you so much.

PS: I love hearing from readers. You can contact me via email at dariowriter@ gmail.com whenever you wish.

ૐ

Some passages in this book originally appeared as blog posts on my own blog, at Janice Hardy's excellent Fiction University *website, and elsewhere on the web. They have been modified and edited (in some cases extensively) for publication here.*

ૐ

Acknowledgments

As always, my sincere thanks are due to a number of people who helped make this book possible. If I've missed anyone, please accept my sincerest apologies. The writing and production of a book takes place over such a span of time and so many processes that sometimes one fails to catch everything.

Huge thanks for beta reading and excellent early input go to my author friends Deborah Jordan Bernal, Aliette de Bodard, Elizabeth Bourne, Jon Del Arroz, Anastasia Poirier, Bonnie Randall, and Gerald Warfield. Thank you all so much.

A big shout-out to the Made in L.A. Writers group which comprises Gabi

Lorino-Tyner, Allison Rose Meek, and Cody Sisco; beyond your individual contributions to this book, I can't tell you all how much I value your support.

There are always a few people who contribute to a book in ways that are hard to pin down, and which may range from simple inspiration to encouragement, faith in you, and hand-holding in those moments of self-doubt which all writers are familiar with. Foremost among these are John Kessel, Ken Liu, Dee Mulligan, Sarah O'Brien, and Kristen Tsetsi.

Last but not least, my greatest thanks of all go to my dear wife Linda, without whose love and support none of this would be possible.

About the Author

Dario Ciriello is a professional author and editor, and the founder (2009) of Panverse Publishing.

Dario's first novel, *Sutherland's Rules,* a crime caper/thriller with a shimmer of the fantastic, was published in 2013. *Free Verse and Other Stories,* a collection of his short Science Fiction work, was released in June 2014.

His 2015 novel, a supernatural suspense thriller titled *Black Easter*, pits love against black magic and demonic possession on a remote, idyllic Greek island. Dario is currently at work on a new thriller.

Dario's nonfiction book, *Aegean Dream*, the bittersweet memoir of a year spent on the small Greek island of Skópelos (the real *Mamma Mia!* island), was an Amazon category #1 for several months in 2012. *The Fiction Writing Handbook: the Professional Author's Guide to Writing Beyond the Rules* (Panverse, May 2019) is his second nonfiction work.

In addition to writing, Dario, who currently lives in the Los Angeles area, offers professional freelance editing, copyediting, and coaching services to indie authors. You can find these on his blog menu at www.dariospeaks. wordpress.com, along with a contact form.

Other Books by Dario Ciriello

Aegean Dream

Sutherland's Rules

Black Easter

Free Verse and Other Stories

Panverse One (editor)

Panverse Two (editor)

Panverse Three (editor)

Eight Against Reality (editor)

Further Resources

There's an ocean of writing books out there, and though I have a whole shelf of them there are only two I would recommend without any reservation as must-haves: these are Stephen King's *On Writing: A Memoir of the Craft* and John Gardner's *The Art of Fiction*.

As well as at least one up-to-date paper dictionary (I'm partial to the *Concise Oxford*), I recommend buying a copy of *The Chicago Manual of Style*, the definitive and invaluable guide to a million questions from which words should be capitalized to when to write numbers as numerals and when to spell them out. I find Strunk and White's classic, *The Elements of Style*, a little dogmatic, but it's still worth owning.

For those who care enough about grammar that they don't mind getting geeky over it, *Warriner's English Language and Composition* is still the gold standard. I'm personally not a thesaurus user, but I do own a *Roget's 21st Century Thesaurus*, and you probably should as well.

On a nuts-and-bolts level, *The Emotion Thesaurus* by Angela Ackerman and Becca Puglisi is extremely helpful when, during revision, you realize that your characters are endlessly nodding and sighing, and that if they don't start exhibiting some variations and subtlety in their body language, your book is likely to be DOA. Unless you're a trained counselor or psychologist, just buy it: it's terrific.

∂ ∂ ∂

Made in United States
Orlando, FL
22 February 2023